ORDINARY PEOPLE EXTRAORDINARY GOD

90 DAYS OF DISCOVERING GOD'S INCREDIBLE WORK IN YOUR DAY-TO-DAY LIFE

A DEVOTIONAL BY MICHELLE MEDLOCK ADAMS, VICTORIA DUERSTOCK, AND OTHERS

END GAME
Press

Library of Congress Control Number: 2023930585
ISBN: 978-1-63797-093-5
eBook ISBN: 978-1-63797-097-3

Cover Design by Abby Chiaradia
Interior Design by Typewriter Creative Co.

Printed in India
10 9 8 7 6 5 4 3 2 1

BEHIND *ORDINARY PEOPLE, EXTRAORDINARY GOD*

When creating a theme for our devotional, we circled back to the same idea each time.

That is, every time we open Scripture—every time we examine our lives—we realize that we have an extraordinary God who chooses to work through unworthy people to bring glory to His name.

Since we at End Game Press have a collection of amazing authors who regularly encourage the people of God through Christian Living books and devotionals, we simply had to join together to explore this idea in a ninety-day devotional format.

Devotional entries are written in order of how the verse appears in Scripture. Our writers pull encouraging examples from several sections of the Bible, from the Old Testament to the New Testament.

We hope that these provide encouragement for your life these next ninety days. And we cannot wait to see how a wonderful God like ours will move and shape your life, dear reader.

THE PATH OF LOGIC OR OBEDIENCE?

Tessa Emily Hall

"Abraham fell facedown; he laughed and said to himself, 'Will a son be born to a man a hundred years old? Will Sarah bear a child at the age of ninety?'"

—Genesis 17:17 (NIV)

When it comes to making decisions—especially big life decisions—we have been conditioned to use calculated judgment. We must consider all factors and possible outcomes. It's common sense, right?

There's nothing wrong with intelligence or common sense … except when it serves as a stumbling block along our path of obedience.

Take Abram, for example. God promised that Abram and Sarai would give birth and that Abram would become the "father of many nations."

But years passed and took their toll on Abram's and Sarai's bodies. Eventually, Abram concluded that his wife was too old to carry a baby. So logic convinced him to take matters into his own hands and sleep with the servant girl instead.

Yet the baby he fathered with Hagar was not the promised son.

In this case, following the path of logic resulted in quite a mess.

You see, God gave us complex minds for a reason—but we must remember that our intelligence is not greater than God's divine power. There may be times when He calls us to do something that just doesn't make sense. It's in these moments that we have a choice.

Will we take the path of obedience or the path of logic?

Both paths involve risk.

Personally, I'd much rather take a chance on the path of obedience. Wouldn't you?

Prayer

Father, Your power exceeds all human wisdom and strength.
Give me the faith I need to take steps of obedience. Amen.

GOOD

Lori Scott

"'You intended to harm me, but God intended it for good to
accomplish what is now being done, the saving of many lives.'"
—Genesis 50:20 (NIV)

Life doesn't always go the way we plan. Illness, injury, divorce, job loss, death, financial strains—no one intends for these situations to happen. But they do.

Several years ago, a broken relationship turned my world upside down. I cried more tears than I knew I had. I got through my heartache by clinging to two thoughts—God loves me. He is faithful.

If both those things were true, then He wasn't surprised by what happened. And He would be right by my side through the whole thing—carrying me if necessary.

God's amazing that way.

Consider the story of Joseph. His brothers sold him into slavery. He was falsely accused of sexual misconduct and thrown into jail. He stayed there for years, separated from his family and stranded in a foreign country. And then, Joseph interpreted the Pharaoh's dream, rose to the second most powerful position in Egypt, and saved thousands of people from starvation—including the very brothers who betrayed him. The story ends well, with a restored family.

Joseph's experience reveals how God can take a situation that looks beyond repair and bring good out of it.

God can do the same for us too. He brings grace out of suffering. Triumph out of tragedy. Healing out of brokenness. Because God's love is bigger than any mess of emotion or injury, we can trust Him when things go wrong (Hebrews 10:23).

Believer, whatever you're facing, you've got this. Because God's got you.

Prayer

Lord, life isn't always perfect. But You are. I know You love me and You are faithful. That's all I need to make it through today. Thank You. Amen.

THE FEAR OF THE LORD

Mary Holloman

"But the midwives feared God and did not do as the king of Egypt commanded them, but let the male children live."

—Exodus 1:17 (ESV)

In the book of Exodus, we see a stark contrast between two worldviews—that of the Pharaoh, and that of two midwives, Shiprah and Puah. The Pharaoh had no fear of the one true God, so he devalued life by ordering the murder of all Hebrew infant boys. But Scripture makes a point of telling us not once, but twice, that the two faithful midwives "feared God." Their steadfast belief in the Author of Life led them to protect the lives of the most vulnerable in the best way they knew how.

Their courageous act of obedience to God saved the life of baby Moses and ultimately led to the deliverance of the Israelites. Because these women valued their Creator, they also valued even the tiniest image-bearers.

Our respect and reverence for God informs our decisions in everyday life. When we recognize that every human being bears the image of our great Creator, we begin to treat others with more love, compassion, and patience. Our fear of the Lord rather than man fills us with courage. Shiprah and Puah may have felt powerless in their positions, but they chose to do what they could, where they could, even if it cost them their lives.

And God used their faithfulness to change the world.

Prayer

Lord, You are the Author of Life, and every human being bears
Your image and Your great name. Help me be faithful and glorify
Your name by treating everyone around me with the dignity, respect,
and compassion they deserve. Help me fear You above all else.

A MOMENT OF COURAGE

Mary Holloman

"Then [Moses'] sister said to Pharaoh's daughter, 'Shall I go and call you a nurse from the Hebrew women to nurse the child for you?' And Pharaoh's daughter said to her, 'Go.' So the girl went and called the child's mother."

—Exodus 2:7–8 (NIV)

There have been many times in my life when I've wondered if my voice matters. In a world where one unpopular word or opinion can get a person "canceled" or ostracized, it sometimes feels safer to keep my viewpoints and convictions to myself. The fear of rejection or the belief that I could never truly make a difference can be paralyzing.

The answer to this fear isn't "I am enough." Rather, it's "God is enough." All throughout Scripture, we see how God uses men and women who are weak, fearful, lowly, or despised in order to bring about His purposes and give Him glory (1 Corinthians 1:27–28).

Nowhere is this more evident than in the life of Miriam. She was not only an enslaved Hebrew but also a female child, making her status unbelievably low. The culture that oppressed her saw her as having little value.

So when she watched from a distance as the daughter of the Pharaoh drew her baby brother out of the water, she had every reason to remain silent. For an enslaved child to approach and speak to royalty could mean severe punishment, or even death. But God used her bravery and boldness as a crucial turning point in the story of His people's deliverance. Her quick thinking allowed Moses' mother to nurse and care for her child—and even be paid for it!

If Miriam had believed the culture's narrative about her own value at the time, she might have allowed fear to keep her silent. But because of her courage, some of her brother's most formative years were spent with his own mother. We can only imagine what Moses' mother was able to teach him about the one true God during her extended time with her son, which could have been anywhere from one to three years.

Miriam had no way of knowing the long-term impact of her split-second decision. But God used her voice in one small moment to bring about His purposes and tell the greater story of His goodness and sovereignty.

Prayer

Lord, give me courage to use the voice You've given me for
Your glory. Help me find my sufficiency in You, not in what
the world says about me. You are enough, always.

WHAT'S THAT IN YOUR HAND?

Victoria Duerstock

"Then Moses answered, "But behold, they will not believe me or listen to my voice … The Lord said to him, "What is that in your hand?" … "that they may believe that the Lord, the God of their fathers, the God of Abraham, the God of Isaac, and the God of Jacob, has appeared to you."

—Exodus 4:1–5 (ESV)

How unique the view of God must be toward our humanity. God sees what we cannot and knows that, despite our failings, He can do something with us when we are willing. This passage is a beautiful reminder that God's power can accomplish far more than we can ask or think when we allow Him to do what He will.

God chose Moses despite his history, despite his doubts, and despite his limits to lead an entire nation out of slavery and into freedom. But He didn't overwhelm Moses with the details. Instead, He told him to tell the Pharaoh to "Let my people go." I often wonder if Moses would have remained brave enough to follow through with the task God had given him to do if he had known fully what the task before him would involve. At each step of the way, God added another layer of responsibility and leadership necessary to accomplish God's purposes.

God in us. The hope of glory. The willingness of one to do what God has said "Do" and go where He says "Go," even in the midst of doubt. There are truly no limits to an obedience that consists of this kind of surrender.

Prayer

Lord, help me today to be willing to do, go, and obey
in the ways You call me today (big or small), knowing
You will do far more than I can even imagine.

YOU CAN'T DO IT ALONE

Josie Siler

"'What you're doing is not good,' Moses's father-in-law said to him.
'You will certainly wear out both yourself and these people who are with
you, because the task is too heavy for you. You can't do it alone.'"

—Exodus 18:17–18 (CSB)

"If you want it done right, do it yourself."

How many times have we heard a version of this quote? I don't know who said it first, but the sentiment has been spoken through the ages. Even Moses tried to do it all. Can you blame him? God called him to the monumental task of leading the Israelites out of Egypt, and he wanted to get it right! It's no small task leading hundreds of thousands of people, but Moses was doing the best he knew how to do.

One day Moses' father-in-law came for a visit and noticed how busy Moses was. The day after Jethro arrived, Moses got back to work judging the people. From morning to night, people came before Moses. I can't even begin to imagine how exhausted Moses was.

Jethro saw it too and asked why he was judging the people alone. He saw that the load was too heavy for one man and suggested a solution.

Moses listened to his father-in-law and divided the labor. Sharing responsibility lifted a heavy burden so that Moses could continue leading the people. If he had continued to do everything himself, he would have crumbled under the weight.

What about you? Are you trying to carry a burden that God never intended for you to carry alone? Are there things you can take off your plate and delegate to others? Is there something you need to share with a friend who will listen and help you bear the weight of your suffering? Do you need to give up control and lay your burdens at the foot of the cross? God never intended for you to do everything yourself!

Prayer

Jesus, I need You. I feel as if I'm about to be crushed under the
load I'm carrying. But You say that Your yoke is easy and Your
burden is light (Matthew 11:30). Help me rest in You. Show me
with whom I can talk and share what's on my heart. I want to walk
with You, Jesus. Thank You for lightening my load. Amen.

PROTESTING A PARENT'S PLANS

Alice H. Murray

"'Why is the Lord bringing us to this land ...?' ... And they said to each other, 'We should choose a leader and go back to Egypt.'"

—Numbers 14:3a, 4 (NIV)

A common interaction in a parent–child relationship is the child resisting a plan their parent has for them. Doesn't the child know what's best? Any parent would answer this question with a resounding "No!" Moms and dads must stick to their guns while their children wail and gnash their teeth and oppose parental plans.

Moaning and groaning from my son reached an all-time high over my plans for him to have a fun experience. I had registered him for church summer camp in a beautiful location. What kid wouldn't want to be away from the parental units with friends for a week "sleeping" in bunk beds, swimming in the lake, and singing around a campfire? Answer: Mine.

Kevin was thrilled with the camp plans until he learned the venue was (GASP!) in another state. That was too far away, so he no longer wanted to go. I tried reasoning with him, pointing out that the camp was only an hour's drive away and just over the state line. Logic made no difference.

Standing firm, I endured whining and complaining from my son the entire way to camp. Vindication came in the end, though. When I picked him up after camp was over, his first words were, "Can I come back next year?" Not only did he attend the same camp each summer for years, but he also worked there as a counselor in his teens.

Father God deals with the same nonsense from His children too. Take the Israelites, for example. God's children refused to trust His extraordinary plans for them in the Promised Land. They grumbled after leaving Egypt and even discussed replacing Moses and returning to the Pharaoh.

While we laugh at the Israelites, aren't we just like them? God plans something wonderful for us, but we resist due to our shortsightedness and spiritual immaturity. If we believe our Heavenly Father loves us, shouldn't we trust His plans for us even when we don't understand or agree with them?

Prayer

Father God, forgive my failure to trust You when You
set me on a path I dislike or don't understand. Help me
to remember the Israelites and not resist. Amen.

A BOLD REQUEST

Josie Siler

"'What Zelophehad's daughters say is correct. You are to give them hereditary property among their father's brothers and transfer their father's inheritance to them. Tell the Israelites: When a man dies without having a son, transfer his inheritance to his daughter.'"

—Numbers 27:7–8 (CSB)

Some things in life just aren't fair. When we run into an unfair situation, we often complain about it, get frustrated with it, and maybe even feel angry. But what if we had the courage to do something about the situation? What if we boldly stepped out of our comfort zone and addressed the issue head-on?

That's exactly what Zelophehad's daughters did. When their father died in the wilderness, the sisters were left with nothing. On top of that, their father had no sons, so his name would die with him. How unfair!

The sisters could have grumbled and complained about how unfair the situation was, but they took a different route. Mahlah, Noah, Hoglah, Milcah, and Tirzah took extraordinary action when they stood at the entrance of the tent of meeting and boldly approached Moses, the priest Eleazar, the leaders of Israel, and the entire community.

What courage!

They explained the situation and made a simple request that they be given property alongside their father's brothers. At the time, this was unheard of. Women simply did not inherit. Yet Moses took their petition to the Lord, and the Lord answered. He told Moses that Zelophehad's daughters were correct—they should be given property and their father's inheritance.

Victory! But the Lord went even further than their request. God instructed the people of Israel that any time a man without a son died, his inheritance should go to his daughter. Because of the bravery of these women, future daughters of Israel were blessed.

The next time you come upon an unfair situation, remember the heroism of Mahlah, Noah, Hoglah, Milcah, and Tirzah and make your own bold request. You never know how many lives your one daring plea may change for the better.

Prayer

Lord, please help me be courageous like Zelophehad's daughters.
You are a good God who wants good things for Your children,
and that includes me. Help me be bold and make this world
a better place to live in for myself and for others. Amen.

HOW CAN I FORGET WHAT THE LORD HAS DONE FOR ME?

Lisa Loraine Baker

"'Only take care, and keep your soul diligently, lest you forget the things that your eyes have seen, and lest they depart from your heart all the days of your life.'"

—Deuteronomy 4:9a (ESV)

Throughout the book of Deuteronomy, God tells His people to remember. Remember what He did for them. Remember His commandments. Remember His mercy and grace. Remember.

My friend Marshall Brandon has seen and experienced more than most. More heartbreak, more sin, more abuse, and most important, more forgiveness. He will be the first to tell you it's not his story, it's God's story in his life. Marshall may remember the depths of his depravity, but his most treasured remembrance is how God saved him.

Marshall erupted from a childhood of abuse and anger and flowed into a life consumed with rage, addiction, and then prison. Somehow, though, he knew he was kept from the worst that could happen. God took his life of destruction and turned it into one of praise.

The moment Marshall surrendered to Jesus, he went back to his old hangouts and said, "You gotta see this! Look at how God can change a sinner like me." Marshall remembered—and he still remembers—what God has done for him. He shares God's work in his life every chance he gets. No one walks away from a conversation with Marshall without hearing about Jesus.

That's his legacy—one of remembrance for what only the Lord can do.

Prayer

Father God, Your kindness overwhelms me and I thank You for Your patience with me, a sinful human. Surrender to You means I am in Your holy hands for whatever You have for me. You are enough, and I will praise You as I remember You, Your word, and Your love. Help me share Your goodness with whomever You place in my path.

WHAT KIND OF WORK CAN WAIT

Lisa Loraine Baker

*"'Observe the Sabbath day, to keep it holy, as the
Lord your God commanded you.'"*

—Deuteronomy 5:12 (ESV)

Sundays are hard for me. Don't get me wrong; I love morning worship with my brothers and sisters in Christ. I enjoy the time spent in prayer, song, and conversations. Sunday school is crammed with lessons from the Bible, so I often fill a journal page or two with observations. We have a solid, biblical pastor, and I add more notes from his sermons.

Sometimes, though, during Sunday school or the sermon, I think about cleaning a closet or dusting the furniture so it's ready for Monday's group Bible study. Argh! Before I know it, I've missed a point I want to transcribe. I make a quick "do this later" note atop my page so I can refocus. Later, I can check to see my do-list atop the sermon notes: *Dust the living room furniture.*

But when I get home—my mind swimming with conversations, prayer requests, and lessons—I push all my *I-gotta-get-this-done-today* tasks to Monday. If no emergency presents itself (like helping a shut-in or fixing a broken window), I long to follow up on what I learned with more time in the word, write messages of comfort and encouragement, and just rest. Good Lord willing, the sun will rise Monday, and so will I. Then I can tackle those duties.

I think the Lord allows our worship service to wear me out so I don't engage in that out-of-focus work I pondered (briefly) during service. At least that's how He works it out with me. I mean, He created us to work. But He also created us to rest, just as He did after the six days of creation. I think on that, breathe a luxurious sigh of relief, and sit on my porch.

Prayer

Father God, thank You for rest. Please forgive me when I
want to cram every day with work. You've given me a day
to rest and reflect on You. Please help me to steward my
time not only with work but also with rest. Amen.

GOD GOES BEFORE YOU

Melanie Redd

"Be strong and courageous. Do not be afraid or terrified because of them, for the Lord your God goes with you; he will never leave you nor forsake you."

—Deuteronomy 31:6 (NIV)

Her name was Jennifer. We were both young moms living in the Atlanta area and attending the same church. From the moment I met Jennifer, I knew we would be friends. She had a sweetness and a depth about her that made her such a precious person. Her laugh was infectious, and she listened with her entire being.

After we had been friends for a while, Jennifer admitted something to me. She told me that when we were both new at our rather large church, she would follow me around at social events. She would let me go first, and then she would sort of hang out just behind me as I'd walk up to people. Once I started a new conversation, she would saunter up and join in.

Because she was rather shy, Jennifer liked for me to go before her into unknown social settings. Over and over, she did this before I ever realized what was going on.

Much like this, we have a God who always goes before us in life. He walks ahead of us and prepares the way for us. Then, he walks with us as well. One of my very favorite quotes on this subject comes from a song by Saint Patrick. A few of the words are as follows: "Christ be with me, Christ within me, Christ behind me and before me. Christ beside me, Christ to win me, Christ to comfort and restore me," (Christ be with me, Prayer of Saint Patrick).

Prayer

Father, remind me that I can do all things today because
You are with me, and You always go before me. I can walk in
confidence and courage today because I never walk alone.

OUTSIDER

Hope Bolinger

"But Rahab the prostitute and her father's household and all who belonged to her, Joshua saved alive. And she has lived in Israel to this day."

—Joshua 6:25 (ESV)

There's something deeply beautiful about the genealogy of Jesus because it contains so many outsiders. So many of Jesus' ancestors—prostitutes, women who had children out of adulterous relationships, non-Israelites—would have made the Israelites at the time blush.

Take Rahab, for instance. She must have endured so many miserable moments. The life of the sex trade can dice apart someone's identity, their hope, their purpose.

Yet God saw this outsider, someone who would sadly be turned out of many places of refuge today, and had a beautiful purpose for her.

Because Rahab had saved the Israelite spies, the Israelites spared her and her family when they invaded Jericho.

Because Rahab had saved the Israelite spies, they allowed her into the community, even though she had Gentile status.

Because Rahab had saved the Israelite spies, her son Boaz married another outsider, Ruth (despite probably knowing the stigma against outsiders).

Because Rahab had saved the Israelite spies, Boaz and Ruth (and Rahab) got grafted into the very genealogy of Jesus.

God loves outsiders. God has a purpose for outsiders.

If you feel as though you don't fit anywhere—in your church, in your small groups, in your community—God sees you, loves you, and has a magnificent plan for you. Remember Rahab, and continue to cling to Him.

Prayer

God, I often feel like an outsider. I don't tend to fit molds well, and can often feel isolated from my community. Remind me of the beauty of Rahab's story—how You redeemed her from horrible circumstances and implemented her into Jesus' own family tree. Amen.

FOR EVERY AGE

Victoria Duerstock

"I was forty years old when Moses the servant of the Lord sent me …
And now, behold, I am this day eighty-five years old. I am still as strong
today… So now give me this hill country … It may be that the Lord
will be with me, and I shall drive them out just as the Lord said."

—Joshua 14:7–12 (ESV)

We find here another story of age not getting in the way of usefulness for God's service. At an age when many are seeking to relax, to step back and let the young people take over, the opposite was true with Caleb. He was one of only two spies who returned believing that they could take the land forty years earlier (though we know that the other spies swayed the people into doubt and disobedience, prompting God to sentence them to wander the wilderness for the next forty years).

We now see that though time passed, Caleb remained no less prepared to walk forward in God's goodness and grace. He requested his share of the Promised Land, knowing that he might face the enemy once again when trying to settle there. Knowing that God would enable him and strengthen him to claim the promise, he continued to walk in obedience as he always had.

As we reach the end of our lives, may we also continue to walk in obedience. May our confidence not waver in the goodness and faithfulness of God just because we are aging. No matter our age, young or old, God has a purpose and call for each one of us to accomplish for Him today!

Prayer

Father, help me to remember that You are capable of great
things within me whether I am eight or eighty-five. Thank
You for the usefulness You find in me, no matter my age.

LEFT-HAND MAN

Hope Bolinger

"Again the Israelites cried out to the Lord, and he gave them a deliverer—Ehud, a left-handed man."

—Judges 3:15 (NIV)

Ever have something so overlooked that it helps you carry out an assassination attempt?

No? Well, Ehud—the left-handed judge of Israel—did.

I love the story of Ehud for so many reasons—the humor, the high stakes, the action, the fact that the king's guards don't check on him because they think he's using the restroom. But one element of the passage in Judges 3 sticks out the most to me: The enemy of Israel never once considered that Ehud might not predominantly use his right hand.

My mom has shared horror stories from her elementary school days when teachers forced her to write right-handed, even though she preferred her left. And I can only imagine the stigma in ancient Israel against lefties.

But God used this overlooked element to carry out His plan. Because the enemy kingdom hadn't expected a left-handed assassin, Ehud passes the initial weapons check and can sneak a long sword into his meeting with the evil king Eglon.

As the story goes, he successfully manages to kill the number one enemy of Israel at the time and makes a daring escape out the porch.

And although we may not find ourselves in high-stakes spy movie situations, we can probably think of an element about ourselves that people often overlook.

How can God make use of what others perceive as a weakness, for His glory? I've found, in life, that nothing goes unused when it comes to the Kingdom of God. If you have a so-called "weakness," ask God how He intends to use it.

Prayer

Heavenly Father, I can point to many areas of my life or personal attributes that others either overlook or perceive as a weakness. Surrendering all that I am to You, I ask that You use my weaknesses as strengths for your Kingdom. Amen.

CHASING GOD

Victoria Duerstock

"Now Deborah, ... was judging Israel at that time. She sent and summoned Barak the son of Abinoam from Kedesh-naphtali and said to him, 'Has not the Lord, the God of Israel, commanded you, 'Go, gather your men at Mount Tabor' ... Barak said to her, 'If you will go with me, I will go, but if you will not go with me, I will not go.'"

—Judges 4:4–9 ESV

Sometimes God uses us in unusual ways. Have you noticed? Deborah, a judge for the nation of Israel, found herself in an odd situation. We know that women were not often found in positions of leadership—in fact, it was unheard of. Yet here was Deborah—judging the nation, doing the work that God had called her to. While we are not privy to all the details of how or why this came about, we know that God used her to lead His people.

Barak had been called by God to go to battle, but he disobeyed. Deborah held him accountable. In that moment, he asked her to go with him, and she agreed. A side lesson here is that if we refuse to go when God sends us, He will find another, more-willing vessel to use for His glory.

While we don't find it in the text, it appears that Deborah never questioned her role; she just moved in obedience to what God had called her to. May we all agree to do the same, despite what it looks like—and despite how it differs from what's normal and acceptable.

Sometimes chasing God doesn't look like we think it will.

Prayer

I pray, dear Lord, that we will follow You faithfully, despite
the circumstances or the challenge to the status quo.

A TENT PEG

Victoria Duerstock

"But Sisera fled away on foot to the tent of Jael ... And Jael came out to meet Sisera and said to him, 'Turn aside, my lord' ... And he said to her, 'Stand at the opening of the tent, and if any man comes and asks you, 'Is anyone here?' say, 'No.' But Jael the wife of Heber took a tent peg and took a hammer in her hand. Then she went softly to him and drove the peg into his temple until it went down into the ground while he was lying fast asleep from weariness. So, he died."

—Judges 4:17–21 (ESV)

I often ponder why some stories make it into the Biblical record and others don't. We know that throughout Scripture, God used His people to accomplish amazing and extraordinary things. One story that did get recorded is that of Jael. Like so many other interesting characters in the Bible, there's not much to know other than this specific story on this day. But what a story it is! God provided rescue for His people at the hands of an ordinary person—a female, no less. In a culture that often belittled females, we find stories of women who carried out the call of God in their lives and changed the course of history.

What led Jael that day to drive the tent stake into Sisera's head, we don't know. But she believed she needed to, no matter the personal risk, so she did.

Often in life, our abilities, our purposes, or our dreams are underestimated. It's easy to become bitter, or outright annoyed, about these underestimations. But those who carry on despite these misconceptions often surprise others with what they accomplish for the kingdom. What really matters in the end is not what others think of us, but rather what we do in obedience to God's call.

Prayer

Father, help me to act in obedience with confidence that You have
a purpose and plan for everything that happens in my life.

NONE OF IT MATTERS WHEN

Victoria Duerstock

"Now the angel of the Lord came and sat under the terebinth at Ophrah, … Gideon was beating out wheat in the winepress to hide it from the Midianites. And the angel of the Lord … said … 'The Lord is with you, O mighty man of valor.'"

— Judges 6:11–16 (ESV)

Beating the wheat was not a glamorous or notable job (though without that work, there would be no bread to eat). But when the angel appeared to Gideon, He called him a mighty man of valor. This is the beauty for me. God sees—and then calls—us for what He knows we can be and will be, *not what we currently are.* God sees so much more deep inside of us, beyond the scope of our vision. He knows that the addition of His calling infused into our nature will, when offered in true submission to His purpose, accomplish His goals!

What a beautiful thing to ponder, my friend. Do you see it?

Our past makes no difference in God's economy. *None of it matters* when He looks on and sees someone that He can use. Someone who will walk forward in faith, believing that if God said it, He will make it come to pass. Someone who recognizes that God's greatness is a beautiful counterpoint to our great weakness, and it is all that is needed—nothing more.

Little is much when God is in it—especially when He is calling me to greater things.

Prayer

Lord, let me be willing—despite my past, my family, or my weakness—to walk in faith, believing that You will use me.

QUALIFIED FOR OUR CALLING

Tessa Emily Hall

"But the Lord said to Samuel, 'Don't judge by his appearance or height, for I have rejected him. The Lord doesn't see things the way you see them. People judge by outward appearance, but the Lord looks at the heart.'"

—1 Samuel 16:7 (NLT)

When Samuel went to anoint one of Jesse's sons to become king, Jesse didn't even take young David into consideration. He showed off his oldest sons instead. I can imagine these older sons were burly. Perhaps they spoke with deep, authoritative voices and had domineering personalities. *They* were the ones who seemed fit to be king.

Not a smelly, teenage shepherd boy.

Aren't you grateful our Lord doesn't judge based on human standards? He doesn't necessarily use the same criteria we do when selecting people for certain positions. He had already qualified David to be king. He chose him to be an ancestor of the Messiah.

Thankfully, God told Samuel not to judge by appearances. So Samuel, with God's nudging, chose the least likely of all to become king.

Nothing other than God's anointing and favor was to be credited.

Personally—as someone who often feels weak and small—this gives me hope. It assures me that, if God has called me to do something for His kingdom, then my lack of physical abilities cannot hold me back. It will be the divine favor of God that qualifies us for our calling.

All for the purpose of expanding His kingdom.

Prayer

Father, many times I've felt unable and inadequate. Yet You have chosen me to fulfill certain roles for the expansion of Your gospel. Give me faith to believe that Your anointing is greater than what I view as my weaknesses. Amen.

BACKSTAGE

Hope Bolinger

"Jonathan took off the robe he was wearing and gave it to David,
along with his tunic, and even his sword, his bow and his belt."

—1 Samuel 18:4 (NIV)

I hate backstage. How do I know? I've spent a great deal of time back there.

As someone whose height stretches past 5'10", I've given many play directors trepidation that I will literally overshadow some people in the cast. This has often earned me a backstage role, where I help to make other actors shine while I move set pieces and pull the curtain.

Such a thing happened during a production of *Tarzan* in high school. My best friend had made the cast; I hadn't. Despite us both spending six months preparing for auditions, the director told me that my height prevented me from earning a part.

So I begrudgingly read my friend her lines, yanked at the curtain, handed props to the actors … huffed in defeat.

Until opening night. In the aftermath of the show, I saw my friend greeting her friends and family in the theater lobby. She'd given glory to God in her bio in the program, and had worked extremely hard to showcase the gifts and talents He'd endowed her with.

After she spoke with them—many of whom weren't believers—she returned to me and squeezed my shoulder. "Thank you for helping me to shine."

It felt like rocks slid down my stomach. Why hadn't I thought of it that way before? Without members of the backstage, those onstage couldn't perform to the best of their abilities.

Jonathan had the same mindset in the Bible. Although he very much deserved the next seat on the throne of Israel, he recognized that God wanted David "onstage" and for Jonathan to play a "backstage" role. Without hesitation, he symbolically transferred his kingship to David. How often do we resent backstage roles because we want all the glory? Let's be more like Jonathan and hand over our kingly robes.

Prayer

Father, I often want the spotlight. I get frustrated when
You place me behind the curtain. Help me to glorify You
no matter where You position me in life. Amen.

AN ABLE GOD

Hope Bolinger

"'There is still a son of Jonathan; he is lame in both feet.'"
—2 Samuel 9:3 (NIV)

Living with a number of disabilities—both physical and mental, often invisible—I often find myself challenging my worth. What if I pass out again at work and have to explain to my employer why I couldn't make it to a weekly meeting? What if I slip into another depression funk and can't will myself to leave the couch, let alone make it to theater practice?

Society lives on ability.

The ability to walk up a flight of stairs. The ability to hear the instructions given on a Zoom or phone call from a potential client. The ability to read the devotional before you without the use of Braille.

But the kingdom of God doesn't operate this way. God can bring glory to Himself in powerful ways through those we perceive as the least powerful people.

Take Mephibosheth, for instance. During the time of David, kings deposed the family members of previous rulers. They would wipe out everyone and anyone who had a distant relation to the former king.

So when David hears about Mephibosheth, the only remaining member of Saul's family, those in David's culture would've expected him to kill off the man who had a disability.

Instead, David invites him to his table. Shares food with him. Gives him his father's land.

Through a man who had a disability, God brought forth reconciliation between two warring families. God shows up for so many more people who have visible and invisible disabilities in Scripture (see Exodus 4:10, Luke 8:43, John 9, etc.).

And surely, if He valued those with disabilities back then, He is willing and able to work through us now—no matter what our ability.

Prayer

Lord, I often question my role in your kingdom based on my
ability, but I know that You don't care about what I can do. Because
You move beyond what I can do to show Your glory. Amen.

MIGHTY MEN

Victoria Duerstock

"And Benaiah the son of Jehoiada was a valiant man of Kabzeel, a doer of great deeds. He struck down two ariels of Moab. He also went down and struck down a lion in a pit on a day when snow had fallen."

—2 Samuel 23:20 (ESV)

Mark Batterson shared thoughts on this passage and on the person of Benaiah in his book *In a Pit with A Lion on a Snowy Day.* It's such an unusual title, I had to read the Biblical account—and that got me hooked on trying to learn more about this man. There isn't much in the Bible about him, except that we know he was one of David's "mighty men."

We can infer from this passage that he was a brave man. Benaiah was someone who trusted and loved God and knew that with God all things were possible. To be honest, I don't know too many people who would willingly get into a pit with a lion on any kind of day, let alone kill one with their bare hands. Benaiah was truly quite remarkable. Although he is not a main character in our Scriptural accounts, I find it interesting that he was such an inspiring character nonetheless.

What a great reminder to us. This is just how so many of those who do Kingdom work are—fairly ordinary people, working to serve, that God chooses to do the extraordinary with. While there's not much glory in doing the things that must be done so others can advance the gospel message, and it can be easy to overlook those in the background doing the ordinary, God never misses a thing. He utilizes it all for our good and His glory.

Prayer

Thank You, Lord, for using me—an ordinary person—
to do what only You can do through me!

ALL I HAVE

Alice H. Murray

"Elisha replied to her, 'How can I help you? Tell me, what do you have in your house?' 'Your servant has nothing there at all,' she said, 'except a small jar of olive oil.'"

—2 Kings 4:2 (NIV)

When life becomes rough, we usually focus on what we don't have. The poor widow in 2 Kings 4 could easily have enumerated things she was missing—including a husband to provide for her, the ability to support herself and her children, and the means to forestall creditors from enslaving her sons for debt repayment. The bottom line? She was in big trouble.

Under these circumstances, what could the woman do? In her distress, she cried out to God's prophet, emphasizing how her husband had revered the Lord. Her spouse was dead and now her two sons were to be taken as slaves.

Elisha's response is puzzling from a human perspective. He asked the distraught woman what she had in her house. Who cares what she had? Didn't Elisha understand that the woman was without a spouse and financial stability while the loss of her sons to slavery loomed?

The widow's answer reflected her confusion at the prophet's question. She didn't have anything; that was the whole point of her seeking assistance. But to emphasize just how little she had, she noted all she had was a *small* jar of olive oil.

But God's perspective is different from ours. To assist the widow, He looked to what she had, not what she didn't. He used her small jar of oil to rescue her. Elisha directed the widow to pour oil from her one small jar and fill all the jars she could find or borrow. And miracle of miracles, the oil didn't run out until every jar she could get her hands on, even ones from neighbors, were full. She went from drowning in debt to overflowing with olive oil to sell to get her out of debt.

Our extraordinary God can use what we have, even if we don't think it's much of anything, to help us. It's not about what we don't have; it's about Who can use what we do have.

Prayer

Dear God, remind me that all I need to have is You.
Let me never forget Your ability to provide for me
even if my resources seem insufficient. Amen.

CARING COMMENT

Alice H. Murray

"She said to her mistress, 'If only my master would see the prophet who is in Samaria! He would cure him of his leprosy.'"

—2 Kings 5:3 (NIV)

Words are powerful. They are so powerful that a well-known proverb states the pen is mightier than the sword. Yet words are not only written but can also be spoken. An ordinary person uttering a few simple words can set into motion events leading to extraordinary action by God.

No one could be more ordinary than the young slave girl from a conquered land serving the mighty Naaman, a highly regarded man and great commander in the King of Aram's army. The slave girl was of no consequence in society, as she had three strikes against her: She was young, female (translation: property), and a foreigner. Her insignificance is emphasized by the fact that she's not even named in this Bible story in which she appears.

Despite her lowly and quite ordinary status, this slave observed Naaman's health issue and cared enough to comment about a solution. Naaman suffered from leprosy, but he could be healed if he would see the prophet in Samaria, she suggested out of concern.

This idea was passed along to Naaman, who brought it to the king's attention. He received permission to travel to see the prophet Elisha. At Elisha's direction, Naaman dipped himself in the Jordan seven times; his flesh was restored and became clean. God miraculously healed Naaman of his dreadful disease, and Naaman declared his recognition that there was no God in the world except in Israel.

Although not detailed in 2 Kings, certainly King Aram was advised of Naaman's miraculous healing, and the event became the talk of the king's subjects. A few caring words from an ordinary young slave girl led Naaman to God's prophet for healing. God's extraordinary healing of Naaman then became known throughout Aram.

Like Naaman's slave girl, we may feel insignificant and incapable of doing anything to serve God. However, sometimes all God wants us to do is to speak caring words that direct another to Him. He can take it from there for extraordinary results—as Naaman could attest.

Prayer

Dear God, thank You for giving us the Living Word, Your Son, Jesus. Guide us to speak caring words that might lead others to You and Your extraordinary love and power.

NO AGE LIMIT

Victoria Duerstock

"Josiah was eight years old when he began to reign, and he reigned thirty-one years in Jerusalem. His mother's name was Jedidah the daughter of Adaiah of Bozkath. And he did what was right in the eyes of the Lord and walked in all the way of David his father, and he did not turn aside to the right or to the left."

—2 Kings 22:1–2 (ESV)

Lest we forget that God can use anyone, the story of Josiah should be one that encourages us all. Josiah didn't have a godly example from his father or grandfather. No long generational line of guidance in following God and obeying His commands. In Scripture, they are noted specifically in prior chapters for *not* following God. Yet that didn't stop Josiah from being the person who broke that cycle and served the Lord well by leading as a king who followed God.

What's most notable, of course, is Josiah's age. At just eight years old, he became king. If that was the end of the story, I think we would still be amazed. But that's not all. As a young man, he chose to follow God by leading an entire nation to remove the sinfulness that had corrupted them. By leading Judah to remove the sinful worship practices that had become entrenched in the nation, Josiah not only obeyed God personally but also served Him corporately. I want so badly to know more of the story—how did the nation accept him as king? How did they react when he changed their worship practices? Did anyone doubt that a young child could lead? But Scripture only gives us part of the story, so we are left to see the results of this obedience and the way God used this devoted young man.

If ever someone could be seen as ordinary, how about an eight-year-old boy? If he, in spite of all these things, could follow the Lord and lead well, what excuse can I possibly have to not be capable of the same?

Prayer

Lord, I thank You that there are no limits—including
our age—to what You can do in us!

THAT ONE THING

Mary Holloman

"When I heard these things, I sat down and wept. For some days
I mourned and fasted and prayed before the God of heaven."

—Nehemiah 1:4 (NIV)

We all have that one thing that keeps us awake at night. It's the thing your brain comes back to again and again. The problem to solve. The wrong to right. The one issue that sticks out above all the rest. Perhaps it began as a concern, but it's lived in your mind and heart so long that it's transformed into a burden, a desire. Nehemiah felt the same way.

After seventy years of exile in Babylon, the remaining Jewish people were finally able to return home. But the Jerusalem waiting for them was in shambles. The wall of the city was broken, and the gate had been burned to the ground. The state of the wall not only left God's people vulnerable to enemies but also pointed to a deeper heart problem—their unfaithfulness and distrust of God.

Nehemiah was distraught. He desperately wanted to see his home restored. But he wasn't a general or prophet or warrior—he was a cupbearer, an aide to the king of Persia. What could he possibly do?

Scripture tells us that Nehemiah wept, fasted, and prayed. As he poured out his heart before the Lord, his burden for the people of God intensified. What began as a concern, God grew into a desire that ultimately moved Nehemiah to action. He boldly led a group of Jews back to Jerusalem, oversaw the reconstruction of the wall, stood courageously against opposition, and united God's people in purpose and passion.

We all have that one thing that keeps us awake at night. Maybe for you, it's young mothers or fathers in your community who need mentorship. Maybe it's a pregnancy resource center that needs volunteers. Maybe it's a local school that serves students who have a high rate of food insecurity.

Whatever that one thing is—don't ignore it. God places burdens on our hearts so that we will step out bravely in faith to make a difference where we are.

Prayer

Lord, please reveal to my heart what my "one thing" is. Break my heart
for what breaks Yours. Give me wisdom and eyes to see the opportunities
You've surrounded me with, so that I can make Your name great.

WHEN THINGS DON'T GO TO PLAN

Hope Bolinger

"Remember me for this also, my God, and show
mercy to me according to your great love."
—Nehemiah 13:22b (NIV)

You may have heard of Nehemiah, but you may be less familiar with Zerubbabel and Ezra. All you need to know is that these three men returned to Israel after a lengthy exile in Babylon.

And these three had big visions for reform in Jerusalem.

One of these reforms looked like returning the Israelites to the Torah practices some had strayed from. Another included building a wall to separate Israel from its enemies. Another was rebuilding the temple.

But as we witness in the books of Ezra and Nehemiah, things didn't always go to plan.

Israelites went back to disobeying laws, and the walls didn't do their job. And the temple was a lot smaller than the previous one. So much so that the elders who remembered the former temple cried out in frustration.

Naturally, this disappointed the three men.

They questioned God and wondered why their plans didn't come to fruition. It certainly seemed like God was asking for these things to be accomplished.

Maybe you've felt a lot like the three men listed above. Like you could've sworn God asked you to do something, but plans fell apart. If that happens, know that you're not alone. Sometimes plans dissolve to show us that God, ultimately, has the best plan possible. Trust Him, and know that He still has your back.

Prayer

God, it frustrates me when plans dissolve. But I know
You ultimately have control over my life. So continue to
give me peace about my current situation. Amen.

AS THIS

Hope Bolinger

"And who knows but that you have come to your
royal position for such a time as this?"

—Esther 4:14 (NIV)

We often focus on Esther in this story. And who can blame us?

Esther, an Israelite orphan, ends up saving the lives of the Jewish people from an evil genocide plot. She uses her position of power to aid those who are oppressed and downtrodden, and she exemplifies grace and godliness in a culture far apart from her own.

No doubt an ordinary person, being used by God for an extraordinary purpose.

But we don't often talk about Mordecai, Esther's cousin, in this story. How he helps to guide Esther in making this decision.

Mordecai encourages her to go to the king, even though certain death awaits her if she has fallen out of favor with her husband—a strange cultural practice of their time.

Right after this verse, Esther relents and ventures into the audience of the king, following Mordecai's urging.

Perhaps you've had to be the Mordecai in someone's life to persuade them to pursue a difficult calling, or to guide them through letting go of the grip of a temptation.

The Holy Spirit often prompts us to be like Mordecai. He may ask us to steer a brother or sister in Christ in the right direction—even if that "direction" means trials ahead.

If you have someone in your life who you feel the Spirit prompting you to talk with about a difficult situation, remember Mordecai's example. This man, who served in the court of the king, helped to prevent a genocide by encouraging Esther. And although God may not be asking us to prevent something of that scale, He may prompt us to help someone through a difficult circumstance.

Prayer

God, I often avoid situations where You ask me to spur a fellow
believer in the right direction. I know he or she is facing a tough
choice—and although I may know what the right answer is, it doesn't
make the decision any easier. Help me to encourage them in the
right ways to follow the path You've set before them. Amen.

JOURNALING WITH JOY!

Lisa Loraine Baker

*"My heart overflows with a pleasing theme; I address my verses
to the King; my tongue is like the pen of a ready scribe."*
—Psalm 45:1 (ESV)

Twelve journals cover a seventeen-year period of my life. If I ever lose one, a $100 reward awaits the person who returns it. You see, God has shown me amazing lessons through His word, and I've endeavored to write each within the journals. To lose one would be akin to losing a priceless treasure. Each of the journals includes stories, lessons, and truths I penned as though a "ready scribe." I can pull an older one off a shelf and remember how the Lord kept me, loved me through adversity, and gave me more than I could ever ask or imagine. It's *His* work in me that is priceless.

And as I reflect on God's messages, I try to think of as many ways to share His lessons as I can—articles, posts, books, white papers, etc. It's with great joy I learn and then share.

A pastor I know declared that when he dies, his journals are to be burned. I don't desire that. I pray for a believer to read what the Lord gave me for their encouragement and growth. And I want the Lord to direct an unbeliever to them so they can read of *His* mighty works in such a life as mine.

For now, I'll keep my nose in His word with pen in hand, ready to write what I learn.

Prayer

Lord, thank You for giving all believers the ability to read about
You in Your word. It's there to equip us for whatever You have
for us to do within Your kingdom so others may give You glory
too. What joy! May what we write in a journal reflect Your work
in us, shining as a light to a lost and dying world. Amen.

YOU ARE BEAUTIFULLY AND WONDERFULLY MADE

Melanie Redd

*"For you created my inmost being; you knit me together in my
mother's womb. I praise you because I am fearfully and wonderfully
made; your works are wonderful, I know that full well. My frame
was not hidden from you when I was made in the secret place,
when I was woven together in the depths of the earth."*
—Psalm 139:13–15 (NIV)

When I think back about my two grandmothers, I'm reminded of the awesome beauty they could create. My dad's mom was a wonderful seamstress. She could do anything with a needle and thread or a sewing machine. Today, our home is filled with beautiful quilts, crocheted items, and needlepoint masterpieces that she created. Her gifts add beauty to the world.

Similarly, my mom's mom was a master gardener. With her green thumb, she could just about grow anything … flowers, vegetables, fruit, and gorgeous trees. However, she was best known for her rose garden. Daily she tended those colorful roses, and they were just beautiful.

Much like the handiwork of my precious grandmothers, you also are a special creation. Father God wonderfully made you in the secret place of your mother's womb. He masterfully crafted you together to be the unique person that you are. As you embrace your beauty (both inside and outside), God will use you to make a difference in the lives of those around you.

You can do what is next in your life because you are beautifully and wonderfully made by Almighty God! Your gifts add beauty to the world!

Prayer

God, would You give me great confidence to enjoy who You
made me to be? Teach me to be comfortable in my own skin,
with my unique gifts, using my special talents and abilities.

PLANS, PURPOSES, AND PROVIDENCE

Felicia Ferguson

"The heart of man plans his way, but the Lord establishes his steps."

—Proverbs 16:9 (ESV)

She was a pastor's daughter who had planned to teach and write for the rest of her life after college graduation. But during her junior year, she met a man and fell in love. They married and moved to Washington, DC, where he became the pastor of a prominent Presbyterian church. Although he was highly respected and well-known in the area, she expected a simple life as a pastor's wife, ministering to the needs in their community while journaling her thoughts and insights with hopes of one day being published. But after thirteen years of marriage, he passed away of a heart attack, and she was left with boxes of his unused sermon notes.

Grieving her loss and uncertain how to move forward, she began to read and delve into the deep biblical truths in her husband's teaching. Deciding these insights needed to be shared rather than discarded or boxed away, she began compiling them into a book. She intended to honor him and his work and to provide a living legacy of his devotion to the faith, but she had no dreams of anything beyond that.

But God.

As her book sold and continued to sell, *Guideposts* contacted her and asked her to write her own work for that publication. Ultimately, she produced over thirty books, which sold more than sixteen million copies. This writing provided her with her own legacy of faith and teaching.

Who was this ordinary woman used so extraordinarily by God? Catherine Marshall. A humble teacher who God transformed into a writer of deep and powerful insights.

As with Catherine Marshall, God has gifted us each with talents that He longs to cultivate for His glory and our growth. We may have some idea or a dream of what we want to do with our lives, but if we hold onto that loosely and give God the space and grace to work His will and plan in us, then we remain open to outcomes from the One who can *"do far more abundantly than all that we ask or think"* (Ephesians 3:20, ESV).

Prayer

Lord, help me to look to You for guidance in
my life as I plan my steps. Amen.

FOCUS ON WHAT MATTERS

Lisa Loraine Baker

*"You keep him in perfect peace whose mind is
stayed on You, because he trusts in You."*

—Isaiah 26:3 (ESV)

I've never seen Shelley without her walking boot. Nor have I seen her without a smile or an encouraging word. The walking boot is to keep a diabetes-induced wound protected so she won't lose her foot. She's already endured diabetic retinopathy, which can cause vision loss and blindness.

Diabetic since she was a child, Shelley has been on kidney dialysis for two years—three times a week, four hours each time. Recently she had surgery to replace an infected infusion port, and now she may do her dialysis at home.

What does a person with such limited energy and physical capabilities do?

During Sunday worship services, Shelley often closes her eyes and sings with a full heart, hands raised in praise to the Lord. She is a prayer warrior. Despite her rigorous, hours-long dialysis treatments, Shelly faithfully attends the weekly prayer meeting. She initiates and oversees many outreach efforts that open hearts to surrender to Christ.

When asked how she's doing, Shelley looks up toward heaven and always answers, "Peachy," and she means it. As she pushes life's problems into the background, she focuses on what matters—Jesus.

Prayer

Lord God, You hold us in ways we may not always acknowledge
or understand. Help us to focus on You and let our trust in You
point others to Jesus Christ, our Peace. We love you and we trust
Your perfect plan. In the matchless name of Jesus, amen.

GOD HOLDS YOUR HAND!

Melanie Redd

"So do not fear, for I am with you; do not be dismayed, for I am your God. I will strengthen you and help you; I will uphold you with my righteous right hand."

—Isaiah 41:10 (NIV)

Yes. It's true. My husband likes to hold my hand. We've been married now for over thirty years, and he still likes to take my hand … in the car, at church, and as we are walking. He says it makes him feel like we are more connected and more in sync when we hold hands. For the most part, he is the one who takes my hand to hold it. And I feel safer and more loved when he does.

Today's verse tells us that God holds our hand. In God's gestures of love and support, He reaches out His right hand and grabs our left hand. Even more, He promises to uphold us and to lift us up as He holds onto us. To hold God's hand is to be loved and be safely guided through life.

If you used your sanctified imagination, you could picture God holding your hand today. As you get your babies dressed and ready for school, He is holding your hand. When you walk into that difficult meeting at school, church, work, or home, He is holding your hand. As you deal with those aging parents or lay that friend to rest in the grave, God holds your hand.

You and I can get through this life, no matter what comes, because we have a God who walks with us and upholds us with His righteous right hand.

Prayer

Father, thank You that You are always with me. Thank You for strengthening me as You hold my hand. I will not fear because You walk with me through it all.

GOD'S WAYS

Josie Siler

"For my thoughts are not your thoughts, and your ways are not my ways.'
This is the Lord's declaration. 'For as heaven is higher than earth, so my
ways are higher than your ways, and my thoughts than your thoughts.'"

—Isaiah 55:8–9 (CSB)

My dad, Randy, has experienced several types of cancer over the years, but nothing as bizarre as the cancers of 2021–2022. Because of past experience, Dad went to the doctor immediately when two lumps developed on his neck. Things happened quickly from there. Within a matter of days many tests had been done, but nothing prepared us for what the doctors told us.

"It's lung cancer," his primary care doctor told him over the phone. A few days later, our family of four got special permission to all cram into a little office to hear the plan from the oncologist. Much to our—and his—surprise, Dad did indeed have lung cancer, but not in his lungs! This type of cancer was so rare they weren't sure how to treat him at first.

They came up with a plan of chemo and radiation and ordered a PET scan. To our surprise, the scan showed a different type of cancer in his kidney. Kidney cancer is deadly and doesn't typically show symptoms until it's too late. We believe God allowed Dad to get lung cancer on his neck to reveal the hidden kidney cancer. Only God can do that!

Dad endured chemo and radiation, and a few months later he had a kidney removed (where they discovered not one, but two types of kidney cancer). Through it all, he pointed others to Jesus. He testified to the goodness of the Lord and all the miracles we had witnessed. He blessed the nurses and doctors and was a bright spot in their day.

We can all be inspired to point others to Jesus during hard times, just like Dad has done through his journeys with cancer. If there's one thing we've learned through this, it's that God's ways are not our ways. His ways are far more creative! Even amid the hard things we face here on earth, God is working. We become a living testimony to the greatness of our God when we acknowledge His work in our lives.

Prayer

Lord, so often I don't understand why You allow me to suffer. I know
You can take my pain away in a moment. Yet I trust that if You're
allowing me to go through something, it's for a reason. I know that You
have a plan for my life, and it's a good plan. Help me to trust You, to
look for the ways You're working in the midst of my suffering, and to
have the courage to tell others what You have done in my life. Amen.

RESTORATION

Lisa Loraine Baker

*"Heal me, Lord, and I will be healed; save me and I
will be saved, for you are the one I praise."*

—Jeremiah 17:14 (NIV)

A tall Indian man named Sanj, whose countenance spoke of a shattered life, asked the church secretary if he could see "that friendly Black pastor." When his assistant told him it was the pastor's day off, the man wept. He left his number and asked that the pastor call him. After the assistant watched Sanj stumble down the hall and out the door, she called Pastor Brandon.

"Please, can you come in and meet this man? I think he's in life-threatening trouble."

"Call him. I'm on my way."

Pastor Brandon recognized Sanj as a recent visitor to the church—the visitor who avoided him on Sundays. When Sanj walked back into Pastor Brandon's office, he slumped into one of the chairs. Pastor Brandon sat in the chair beside Sanj and listened as Sanj shared his sad journey into worldly financial success and selfish pride. He told the pastor he'd ruined his marriage and his life, and when he received the call from the pastor's assistant, he was on his way to commit suicide.

Pastor Brandon and Sanj talked for a while. He told Sanj about our Savior, Jesus Christ, and how He lives so we, too, can live. He told him every life is precious and that God could use Sanj's for His glory—even his broken life. The pastor assured the visitor that as long as we have breath, there is always hope. Then he asked Sanj if he would like to surrender to Jesus and be His child.

When Pastor Brandon buzzed his assistant and asked for a new believer's Bible, she wept joyfully. She knew the outcome of Sanj's visit. As she entered his office, both men were in tears, and as Sanj stood, the weight of his former life was gone, replaced by joy.

The Lord drew Sanj to Himself and changed his life. His marriage was restored, and he dedicated his life to serving Jesus.

Prayer

Lord Jesus, thank You for not leaving us where You find us. Our trials
are but a foreshadow of those we will face as Christians, but the weight
of eternal glory makes them pale in comparison. As You restore us, use
everything we've encountered to bring glory to Your name. Amen.

GOD HAS GREAT PLANS FOR YOUR FUTURE!

Melanie Redd

"'For I know the plans I have for you,'" declares the Lord, "'plans to prosper you and not to harm you, plans to give you hope and a future.'"

—Jeremiah 29:11 (NIV)

It's one of the most commonly asked questions in my ministry. Women, teenagers, college students, and several close friends have asked the question this year. It comes in various forms, but the gist of it is this ... "How do I know that God has great plans ahead for my life?"

It is a wonderful question. A fair one for sure. And my answer is always the same. I quote today's verse and then remind my friends that God promises to have plans for our lives. His plans are good, offering us a hope and a future. They are plans to prosper us and not to harm us. I believe this with all of my heart because the Bible tells us it is so.

Next, inquiring minds want to know how they can experience God's good plans for their lives. My answer to this question is not complicated either.

Typically, I will give them a short list of ways to get in on God's will: 1) Pray and ask God to lead you. 2) Open the Bible and begin to read. Start in Proverbs. 3) Invite your wise friends and mentors to share their insights. 4) Do all you know to do. Do the next things you know to do. 5) Watch for God to open the doors and line things up for you.

To know God's will, we must press in close to Him and ask Him to reveal His plans to us. We know God's plans by getting to know God. Seek His heart and then you will see His plans.

Prayer

Lord, thank You that I can face the future because I know You
have amazing plans for my future. Help me to push in really
close to You and discover more of what You have for me.

THE GOD OF ABUNDANCE

Tessa Emily Hall

"'O Sovereign Lord! You made the heavens and earth by your strong hand and powerful arm. Nothing is too hard for you!'"
—Jeremiah 32:17 (NLT)

I grew up in South Carolina where the skies could show off their starry beauty without the disruption of big city lights. On nights when the skies were especially dazzling with diamonds, my mom would take me out into the driveway and point upward. "Our Heavenly Father was the One who created that. His abundance and resources are unlimited!"

These words came back to mind the other day when I arrived home at midnight. I was returning from a trip—one that was filled with God's favor and answered prayers. As I stepped out of the car, I gazed in awe at the starry sky as it projected God's endless power.

I knew, in that moment, that my mom was right. As children of God, we don't need to be held back by what seems impossible. Or by our weaknesses, failures, or shortcomings.

See, we serve a good Father. And good fathers don't hoard their resources for themselves;

rather, it is their joy to bless and provide for their children. Not because their children earned it. No, their fatherly love is unconditional.

Still, earthly fathers are limited in what they can offer their children. Our Heavenly Father, however, is not. His resources, power, and abundance are endless.

And it is His heart's delight to share that with His children.

Prayer

Thank You, Lord, for being a good Father. I can't rely on myself and my own abilities because I am limited by my human nature. That's why I depend on You and Your strength, power, and resources. Thank You for the many ways You have already shared that with me. Amen.

JUST DO YOUR JOB

Alice H. Murray

"He ordered the furnace heated seven times hotter than usual and commanded some of the strongest soldiers in his army to tie up Shadrach, Meshach and Abednego and throw them into the blazing furnace."

—Daniel 3:19b–20 (NIV)

Some biblical characters undertook awesome tasks. Noah built an ark, Moses led the Israelites out of Egypt, and David killed Goliath using a slingshot. But God's ends can also be attained when humans perform ordinary tasks—like simply doing their jobs.

The story of the fiery furnace illustrates how merely fulfilling the role we've been given may pave the way for God to achieve extraordinary results. It is not only a gripping tale but also a good lesson on how God works.

According to the biblical narrative, King Nebuchadnezzar ordered that a gigantic golden statue be made for all to bow to. Refusal came at a cost—death. And execution wouldn't be quick and painless; the condemned would be burned alive in a blazing furnace.

But how did those who were sentenced to death get into the furnace? Enter King

Nebuchadnezzar's soldiers. In Daniel 3, the strongest men in the king's army were directed to tie up Shadrach, Meshach, and Abednego and pitch them into the fire. Without those unnamed soldiers carrying out their orders, the story wouldn't have progressed. And just by doing their jobs, these men set the scene for God to stage a miraculous intervention, deliver the condemned from death, and exhibit His might to the king and the Babylonian empire.

Often, we perceive ourselves as not being useful to God because we cannot accomplish something spectacular like Noah, Moses, and David did. "All" we can do is fulfill the role we've been given. But isn't that the point God is trying to make? It's not what great things we can do for Him, but what extraordinary things He can do through us. Sometimes what He requires is for us to do what we are supposed to be doing right where He's placed us. Let's do our jobs and leave the extraordinary results to Him.

Prayer

Dear God, help me focus on what You can accomplish. Allow me to
realize You can use my ordinary acts for your extraordinary ends. Amen.

ONCE UPON A DREAM

Hope Bolinger

"And afterward, I will pour out my Spirit on all people.
Your sons and daughters will prophesy, your old men will
dream dreams, your young men will see visions."

—Joel 2:28 (NIV)

I love how we have a God who moves through dreams.

And I don't just mean the goals we strive to achieve. Although I will never forget what Michelle Medlock Adams often says ("God never forgets a dream"). It's true. He doesn't.

But God has, in the past, moved through the *literal* dreams of people. Even when we fall asleep idle, God continues to work. Daniel saw visions of the future. Joseph received a dream that told him to move Mary and Jesus to Egypt before Herod could slaughter their child. The list goes on.

God even moves in dreams today. We hear stories overseas of people—who have never encountered the Bible—seeing Jesus in dreams. They then want to know more, and commit their lives to the Lord.

We have a God who is always working, a God who meets us in our dreams and in our waking. Praise God that He moves in all circumstances.

Prayer

Heavenly Father, You never cease to work in our lives.
Whether or not I have seen visions or dreams, I know You
move in extraordinary ways to meet people where they're at.
Continue to work through us as we await You. Amen.

BEARER OF BAD NEWS

Hope Bolinger

*"The pride of thine heart hath deceived thee, thou that dwellest
in the clefts of the rock, whose habitation is high; that saith in
his heart, 'Who shall bring me down to the ground?'"*

—Obadiah 1:3 (KJV)

List some of your favorite prophets of the Bible. Go! Did you mention Elijah? Maybe Daniel and his famous adventure in the lion's den? Perhaps you thought of Jeremiah or John the Baptist or even Elijah's protégé Elisha.

I'm going to hazard a guess—unless you cheated and looked at the verse in this devotional—that you didn't mention Obadiah. And I can't blame you. Obadiah only spends one chapter in the Bible, and he doesn't take any time to introduce himself. Or have much of anything joyful to say. Instead he spends most of his time condemning one of Israel's enemies, Edom.

So why even mention him? Why does his book get included as one of the thirty-nine of the Old Testament? I would love to mention two possible reasons why we should pay attention to this minor prophet.

First, we cannot understand the love of God unless we understand the judgment of God. Edom had swelled with pride, and a simple "You be you" message wasn't going to cut it with these people. They needed to comprehend that their actions against the people of God had consequences—spiritual consequences, as they'd steeped themselves in sin.

Second, as ordinary people being moved by an extraordinary God, we sometimes have to be the bearers of bad news. We have to tell a believer that their gossiping isn't benefiting the kingdom. That our brother or sister who is dwelling in sin is diving into some pretty scary territory, spiritually speaking. We speak these truths in love, but we speak the truth nonetheless. And sometimes doing that is what can turn ordinary conversations to extraordinary ones.

Prayer

Father, help me to speak the truth in love. Sometimes You
call me to be the bearer of bad news. Help me to do so in
a loving manner that points others to You. Amen.

GOD SINGS OVER YOU

Melanie Redd

"'The Lord your God is with you, the Mighty Warrior who saves. He will take great delight in you; in his love he will no longer rebuke you, but will rejoice over you with singing.'"

—Zephaniah 3:17 (NIV)

As we stood in front of a large gathering of friends and family members, my soon-to-be husband sang to me. Randy used his beautiful tenor voice to express his love for me on the day of our wedding, and he's been singing to me ever since—for over thirty years now. I never tire of hearing him sing, especially when he is singing to me, to our kids, or to Jesus.

When our children were babies, my husband would make up little songs to sing to them. He would sing to them as he changed their diapers, fed them, rocked them, or walked them. Some of their first memories were of hearing their daddy sing over them.

Have you ever thought about the fact that God sings over you? I think He probably has a deep bass voice. But whatever He sounds like, He's perfectly in tune, right on key. And His songs are sung with incredible delight, joy, love, and compassion.

Perhaps today He is singing to you to remind you not to be afraid. Or maybe His song is one of celebrating a big accomplishment or an answered prayer. God may be singing a quiet song reminding you He is right beside you today. Or He could be singing a song to comfort you during this particularly hurtful or lonely season. Listen closely. Can you hear Him?

Prayer

Lord, would You help me to listen closely today, knowing You
are singing over me? As I walk through the events of this day,
I want to enjoy Your presence and Your songs to me.

I CHOOSE YOU, GOD

Josie Siler

"But seek first the kingdom of God and his righteousness, and all these things will be provided for you. Therefore don't worry about tomorrow, because tomorrow will worry about itself. Each day has enough trouble of its own."

—Matthew 6:33–34 (CSB)

Erin Elizabeth Austin is thankful to be alive ten years longer than doctors expected. Diagnosed with lupus, fibromyalgia, and Crohn's disease, she has suffered greatly for many years. She's prayed for healing and has gotten it in small measures, but she's never had full physical healing.

Through her years of suffering with chronic illness, Erin has grown closer to the Lord. She's learned things that can't be learned from a book, but must be experienced. She has experienced the peace of God when outwardly she felt like she was wasting away. There were nights she didn't think she would see the morning this side of Heaven.

Even so, Erin knew God had a plan for her life, and she desired to minister to others. She founded Broken but Priceless Ministries in 2010 to encourage people with chronic illnesses as well as caregivers. Erin wants people to know that even though our bodies may be broken, we are priceless in God's eyes.

It's a message Erin has had to learn for herself over the years. God has done a great work in Erin's life. Even though full physical healing here on earth would be amazing, it's not her primary goal. She's come to the point in her walk with the Lord where she would rather know the Healer than receive the healing.

She's learned that even though there are a lot of things she could worry about, she doesn't have to worry about tomorrow. Her heart's desire is to seek first the kingdom of God and His righteousness. We can learn from Erin Elizabeth Austin to seek the Lord above all else. When we do, we'll see that He is all we need. There is trouble in the world, but we can experience peace in God through a relationship with Him.

Prayer

Lord God, I'm not going to lie, there is a lot to worry about. There
are so many unknowns in life, but You know everything! You go
before me and You make a way where there seems like there couldn't
possibly be a way forward. I know, like the Apostle Paul wrote in
Philippians 1:21, that to live is Christ and to die is gain. There
is nothing to fear when I walk with You, Lord. Help me to seek
You first. Help me to keep my eyes on You and to not worry about
things I can't control. I love You, Lord, and I choose You! Amen.

JUST ASK GOD

Alice H. Murray

"Jesus said, 'Let the little children come to me, and do not hinder them, for the kingdom of heaven belongs to such as these.'"
—Matthew 19:14 (NIV)

The preschool playground buzzed with excitement. The youngsters were especially pumped up today. They were aware Christmas was approaching, which would bring much-desired toys and clothes—perhaps even a bike.

Their teacher stood off to the side, keeping a watchful eye on her little charges. Her reserved demeanor indicated not only that she was an adult, but also that the looming holiday was not anticipated with great expectation. She knew she would not receive what she wanted most.

A small girl bounded up to her teacher. "What do you want for Christmas?" the student asked. Since it was a Christian preschool, the teacher concluded honesty was the best policy. "My husband and I would really like to have a baby."

Immediately the youngster responded, "If you want a baby, you need to ask God for one." She then dropped to her knees right there on the playground, clasped her little hands together, and closed her eyes. "Dear God, please bring my teacher a baby for Christmas." Prayer completed, the girl arose and scampered off to rejoin her classmates.

While impressed with her student's faith, the teacher wasn't holding her breath that she would receive a bundle of joy for Christmas. Nevertheless, not two weeks later she and her husband found themselves in a hospital on Christmas Eve, taking placement of a newborn they were going to adopt. The situation had dropped into their laps just a couple of days beforehand. The teacher knew this result could be attributable to only one thing—the simple prayer of a child asking God to give her teacher what she wanted for Christmas.

No wonder Jesus directed that the little children be allowed to come to Him. Ordinary youngsters grasp the concept of asking and receiving from their Heavenly Father. By asking, this sweet preschooler set the stage for an extraordinary result. Her teacher believed the infant she and her husband held in their arms on Christmas was God's undeniable answer to the student's prayer. Oh, that we all could have the faith of that young child.

Prayer

Dear God, allow me to believe as a small child—and to ask of
You with full belief that You will answer my prayer. Amen.

THE LORD NEEDS IT

Alice H. Murray

"If anyone says anything to you, say that the Lord needs
them, and he will send them right away."

—Matthew 21:3 (NIV)

God is the Almighty, the Creator of our world. He is all-powerful. What could He possibly need from humans?

From the beginning of the Bible, we see God desires a relationship with humans. He wants us to partner with Him to achieve His purposes. Adam, for example, was tasked with being a steward of the Garden of Eden. While Adam's assistance was not required for God to keep things in order in this earthly paradise, his participation was necessary for a relationship between God and His creation.

But Genesis is in the Old Testament, and Adam (as the first man) was special. What can ordinary humans contribute to a partnership with God?

The story of Palm Sunday offers a wonderful example of a human working with God. Other than palms and Jesus, a key part of this event is the mode of transportation Jesus used to enter Jerusalem—a donkey. But Jesus was an itinerant teacher who walked everywhere. He didn't own a donkey.

God could have simply placed a donkey to use near Jesus. Instead, God called upon a man the disciples met on the streets of Jerusalem to supply what was needed.

The disciples approached the donkey owner and stated the Lord needed it. The man responded by relinquishing his animal. And his animal famously became a part of the story of Holy Week, allowing Zechariah's prophecy about the Messiah coming to His people riding on a donkey to be fulfilled.

While the donkey's owner isn't named in the Gospels, he illustrates how an ordinary person can partner with God by willingly giving what God requests of them. In the Palm Sunday story, a donkey was requested. For us, God may ask for our time, our talent, or our financial resources.

God will take whatever He requests of us and use it for His greater glory. He allows ordinary people the opportunity to partner with Him by giving Him what He requests of them for His extraordinary purposes.

Prayer

God, thank You for allowing me to be a part of Your
wonderful plans. Open my heart to be willing to surrender
whatever You ask for to further them. Amen.

A LEAP OF FAITH

Josie Siler

*"And the King will answer them, 'Truly I tell you, whatever you did for
one of the least of these brothers and sisters of mine, you did for me.'"*
—Matthew 25:40 (CSB)

Sometimes we hear something that we can't *un*hear. It stays with us and we must act. That's exactly what happened to Jenny Almquist when she first learned about the horrors of sex trafficking—and that it's everywhere, even in rural Wisconsin.

The thought appalled Jenny, and she had to do something. She started by creating a business called Fierce Beauty. She sold beautiful scarves and donated a portion of the proceeds to nonprofits who were fighting human trafficking. She had parties, went to craft shows, and eventually started an online store so people could shop from anywhere.

Soon that wasn't enough. As Jenny learned more about the human trafficking industry and saw the impact it was having in the rural area and small towns near her, she wanted to do more. She founded a nonprofit called Fierce Freedom, which is now making a huge impact in western Wisconsin. The organization's mission is *empowering through education.*

Members provide training on their website, but they also train first responders and go into churches, schools, and community groups to train members and raise awareness. They speak at events and even have a podcast so they can reach a broader audience. They've rescued people who have been trafficked, and they have many resources on their website for people who are looking to help or find help.

Jesus said, *"Whatever you did for one of the least of these brothers and sisters of mine, you did for me"* (Matthew 25:40). We don't need to know everything to help someone in need. Jenny took a huge leap of faith and learned as she moved forward in obedience to what God called her to do. We can find the courage to step out in faith just like Jenny did when she learned the horrors of human trafficking and decided to do something about it. God calls us to different things. Where is He asking you to step out in faith?

Prayer

Lord, I know what You're asking me to do, but I'm afraid. I don't know how to do what You've called me to do, yet I trust You. I know that You will help me when I take that leap of faith, so I'm leaping, Lord. I choose to follow You and trust You on this journey we're taking together. And when something good happens, I know it will be You working through me. Thank You, Lord, for never asking me to do something on my own. Thank You for being right there with me every step of the way. Amen.

GOD WILL MEET YOU WHERE YOU ARE

Michelle Medlock Adams

"Jesus said to him, 'If you can believe, all things are possible to him who believes. Immediately the father of the child cried out and said with tears, 'Lord, I believe; help my unbelief!'"

—Mark 9:23–24 (NKJV)

I love this story in Mark 9 because it shows that God will meet us wherever we are as long as our hearts are toward Him. Remember the story? A man whose son is demon-possessed comes to Jesus for a miracle. He tells him all the details concerning his son's situation—he can't talk, he has seizures and foams at the mouth, he gnashes his teeth. Jesus asks the father, "How long has he been like this?" The man answers, "From childhood," stating the demon has thrown his son into the fire and into the water to try and kill him. And then the father pleads, "If you can do anything, take pity on us and help us" (Mark 9:21–22).

Jesus doesn't get offended. He simply says, "All things are possible to him who believes."

Then, here's my favorite part of the story. The father cries out to Jesus, "Lord, I believe; help my unbelief!"

Talk about honesty! That father laid it all on the line, and Jesus delivered the boy. You see, there's power in vulnerability.

I've often found myself saying, "Lord, I believe! Help my unbelief!" And the Lord doesn't turn away from me in disappointment. He meets me right where I am. Jesus knows our hearts—He understands when we are trying to believe, but doubts are creeping in and trying to crush our faith. He doesn't condemn us when we cry out, "I believe; help my unbelief!" No, He is happy that we cried out to Him. So let's stop pretending to believe, and instead ask God to help our unbelief during those seasons of doubt. He will. The Bible says we have not because we ask not, so ask (James 4:2).

Prayer

Father God, thank You for loving me even when I have doubts.
Thank You for meeting me right where I am. I'm asking
today: Help my unbelief. I trust You, God. Amen.

WHAT DO YOU WANT?

Josie Siler

*"He threw off his coat, jumped up, and came to Jesus. Then
Jesus answered him, 'What do you want me to do for you?'*
'Rabboni,' *the blind man said to him, 'I want to see.'"*

—Mark 10:50–51 (CSB, emphasis mine)

My grandma loved sugar cookies. I remember times when she really wanted them, but she didn't want to ask us to bring her some. She would hint around, hem and haw, but never ask. Finally, she'd cave and ask for her beloved sugar cookies. We all knew what she wanted, and often we did bring her cookies without being asked. But sometimes, it turned into a bit of a game and we'd hold out until she asked.

If you have children, you've probably done the same thing. You know what they want, but you want to be asked. There's something beautiful in the asking. Isn't that what God wants from us too? We can take a lesson from Bartimaeus. He was a man who encountered Jesus, persisted in getting His attention, and was honest about what He wanted Jesus to do for Him.

When Jesus left Jericho, there was a large crowd with Him. Bartimaeus was sitting by the road and heard the commotion. When He heard Jesus was passing by, he called out to Him. People told him to keep quiet, but he cried out all the more. When Jesus stopped and called him over, Bartimaeus didn't waste any time. He threw off his coat, jumped up, and came to Jesus.

"What do you want me to do for you?"

"Rabboni, *I want to see."*

Jesus immediately restored his sight, and Bartimaeus followed Jesus. What an example for us! It's humbling to tell God what we want. After all, He already knows what we need. Why should we have to ask? It's all about relationship. He wants us to share with Him the desires of our hearts. He also wants us to think through our motives and what we really need. What do you want God to do for you?

Prayer

Dear Lord, You know the desires of my heart. You know what I long for and what I'm struggling with. It's humbling to admit that I don't have it all together and that I need You. But I do need You, God. I need You to… *(Keep talking to the Lord. Tell Him what you want.)* Amen.

THE PURPOSE OF THESE MIRACLES

Tessa Emily Hall

"The angel replied, 'The Holy Spirit will come upon you, and the power of the Most High will overshadow you. So the baby to be born will be holy, and he will be called the Son of God.'"

—Luke 1:35 (NLT)

What if Mary's attitude had been prideful instead of humble? Rather than be in awe of the miracle God performed in her womb, what if she had boasted about it instead?

Thankfully, she knew it was only through the Holy Spirit that the child was conceived. The impossible nature of this situation served to confirm that this was a work of God.

A few decades later, crowds gathered to watch as Jesus, a humble carpenter, performed miracle after miracle.

Those events also confirmed the truth that He was the Messiah.

Similarly, what if the miracles we've received were intended not only to bless us but also to bless others? And what if God redeemed you out of darkness not only to rescue you, but also so others can witness the evidence of His power?

The purpose of these miracles, then, is so that *God* would receive glory rather than ourselves.

Perhaps this is why He often chooses the weak, ordinary, sinful, and outcast to proclaim His greatness ... so others can watch and be amazed at the impossible transformations. Then they will know, without a doubt, that these miracles couldn't have occurred by any earthly strength or intelligence.

Rather, they occurred only by the supernatural hand of a loving Father.

Prayer

Father, thank You for the many miracles You have performed
in me and through me. I pray that these testimonies will
serve as evidence of Your power and love. Use these miracles
to usher more souls into Your kingdom. Amen.

WHAT ARE YOU HUNGRY FOR?

Lisa Loraine Baker

"And Jesus answered him, 'It is written, 'Man shall not live by bread alone.'"

—Luke 4:4 (ESV)

Pastor Chet came to faith in 1972 when he attended a Billy Graham crusade. He became a pastor in 1982, and his life passage is Jeremiah 9:23–24. When an unknown malady struck him, so did fear—not fear of death, but fear of lasting past his usefulness. He shared his life verse anew with his congregation after having been absent from the pulpit for ten weeks. (He'd been enduring medical tests he never thought probable because he was sure he'd "drop dead," as he says, from a heart attack—just like his father and uncles.)

His weight began a slow descent in January of that year and progressed with frightening rapidity once spring arrived. By the time he spoke to his beloved congregation that August, his body had suffered the loss of over fifty pounds. Anemia from bleeding ulcers was discovered and halted, yet his weight continued its regress, while his energy roller-coastered. As he walked the path to every kind of "ologist," he lost his taste for many kinds of food, including his favorites.

Beloved family and friends, shocked at his appearance and weakness, cried in prayer over him. But Pastor Chet lost more than weight. Through his trial, his faith grew and he lost his fear. What he gained was a renewed hunger to know Jesus as best he can, and he longs to share that passion. He remains steadfast in his faith, and he eschews prayers for healing because he knows his hunger to know Jesus more will be satisfied when he sees Him face-to-face. We should know what Pastor Chet knows—our hunger to know Jesus is the best food we will ever ingest.

Prayer

Lord Jesus, Your word says we are to boast in understanding and knowing You. We do not live by bread alone, which satisfies our physical needs. We live for You, and You are the bread of life who satisfies our every spiritual need and longing. Help us to crave Your word, which brings life everlasting. In Your matchless name we pray, Amen.

COME TO ME

Alice H. Murray

"When Jesus saw her, he called her forward and said to her,
'Woman, you are set free from your infirmity.'"
—Luke 13:12 (NIV)

It was a Sabbath like any other. God's chosen people gathered in their local synagogue as usual. The worship routine included teaching.

Today a guest teacher, a traveling rabbi, filled the teaching slot. What portion of the Torah did He use for His lesson? No one knows. But the action He took is recorded in Luke.

Among the crowd that day stood a crippled woman. *Stood* isn't an accurate description because she was bent over and could not straighten herself. This physical disability had troubled her for eighteen years. Resigned to her infirmity, she went about life as best she could, even making the effort to attend services to worship her Creator.

The teacher, Jesus, noticed the afflicted woman. His focus shifted from teaching using words to teaching a lesson by His actions. He called the woman forward to where He stood.

The woman feared it might be too difficult and embarrassing to make her way to where the teacher waited. Something about Him, though, drew her to Him. Despite her physical limitations and everyone's eyes on her, she answered the teacher's invitation and went to Him.

Her reward for doing something as simple as moving from Point A to Point B in the synagogue? Healing through the amazing words Jesus spoke to her: *"Woman, you are set free from your infirmity."* With His hands on her, she could at once stand straight up. Her almost two-decades-long struggle with being crippled was over. Hallelujah!

The woman's response to Jesus' summons allowed a miracle in her life. An ordinary reaction (come when called) put the crippled woman in the position for Jesus to do something extraordinary—free her from debilitating circumstances. But she had to come to Him to receive that result.

Jesus calls all people to come to Him. In fact, He's offered a standing invitation. If you simply respond and come as He bids, you too will receive something extraordinary—freedom from the infirmity of sin.

Prayer

Dear God, I hear You calling me. I come to
You for release from my sin. Amen.

MORE THAN ALL OF THEM

Josie Siler

"He looked up and saw the rich dropping their offerings into the temple treasury. He also saw a poor widow dropping in two tiny coins. 'Truly I tell you,' he said, 'this poor widow has put in more than all of them. For all these people have put in gifts out of their surplus, but she out of her poverty has put in all she had to live on.'"

—Luke 21:1–4 (CSB)

Remember when we used to pass the offering plate in church? (You know, back before the COVID-19 pandemic changed how we do so many things.) Sometimes it was hard not to notice when someone dropped in a large wad of cash. Other times I'd notice the amount of a check when I dropped in a few small bills. I tried not to compare myself with others, but I have to admit there were times I wondered what good my meager offering did. Some days my small sacrifice felt small indeed. But I never stopped giving what I could because I knew the story of the poor widow. Do you know her story?

It's just a few lines in Scripture, but those lines make a big impact. I can just imagine

Jesus sitting in the temple, surrounded by eager disciples hanging on every word. Jesus looks up and sees rich person after rich person dropping large amounts of money into the temple treasury. But then His gaze lands on a poor widow. He watches her drop in two tiny coins.

She must have felt small compared to the others and their large amounts. Yet Jesus saw her. I imagine Him locking eyes with her while telling his followers to take note of the incredible thing she did. She gave all she had, and that counted more than the largest offering. I believe her small offering showed Jesus that her heart was all His.

Jesus sees you too. Your sacrifices don't go unnoticed. The little you give with all your heart is worth more than an abundance given out of obligation or for show.

Prayer

Jesus, You know my heart. You know how much I love You.
Whether I have much or little, it's Yours. I give You my resources,
my time, my talent, and my love. I give You all of me because
You have given me all of You. Thank You, Jesus! Amen.

LEND ME YOUR EAR

Alice H. Murray

*"But Jesus answered, 'No more of this!' And he
touched the man's ear and healed him."*

—Luke 22:51 (NIV)

In a drama, the spotlight focuses on the main characters in any scene. The supporting cast in the shadows is given a mere passing glance, but without those actors, the plotline may not move forward. Even in the Bible, a supporting cast member can play a pivotal role in a dramatic scene.

What could be more dramatic than Jesus' arrest in the Garden of Gethsemane? God's Son, who has been weeping to the point of shedding drops of blood, is confronted by an armed contingent sent to arrest Him. Judas betrays Jesus, and the disciples cower in fear.

Off to the side of this unfolding drama stands Malchus, a servant of the Jewish high priest. He's present because his master ordered it. What Malchus thinks about Jesus and Jesus' identity is irrelevant. He's merely following orders to be there.

Talk about being in the wrong place at the wrong time. Malchus is suddenly front and center in this drama when Peter, overcome by emotion, draws a sword and wields it wildly. Peter's feeble efforts to protect Jesus result in the loss of Malchus' right ear.

In the middle of this chaos, Jesus turns his attention to the injured servant. He picks up the severed ear and returns it to Malchus' head. Miraculously, the ear is reattached. Malchus, simply by his presence, has set the stage for Jesus to perform His last miracle prior to His crucifixion.

In our lives, we may not have central roles such as pastoring a church or a serving as a missionary in a foreign field. Sometimes God uses us right where we are, like He did with Malchus. Our part could be to serve as a supporting cast member—available for God to work through us. While our role may not be as dramatic as having a body part severed, God can use our presence in a situation for His glory. Will you lend Him your ear?

Prayer

Dear God, help me to recognize that serving You does not
always involve dramatic action on my part. Allow me to
be available for You to use in any life scene. Amen.

NO MORE "FITTING IN"

Tessa Emily Hall

"'Nazareth!' exclaimed Nathanael. 'Can anything good come from Nazareth?' 'Come and see for yourself,' Philip replied."

—John 1:46 (NLT)

I thought popularity contests would end once I graduated high school. Little did I know that they continued throughout life—even among Christians.

Society competes over who wears the best wardrobe ... who has the most friends and social media followers ... who has the most well-behaved kids, the nicest cars, the best-looking husband ... and on and on.

The pressure to fit in is nothing new. Even back in Jesus' day, society segregated people according to their social and economic status.

But Jesus came to tear down those walls of segregation.

His life was the evidence. Jesus Himself was not popular in the eyes of men, yet He modeled for us that man's approval is far different from God's approval.

God uses the humble-hearted—those who serve Him—to shame the wise. He doesn't judge us the way society tends to judge.

This means that we can relent in our efforts to fit in. Our efforts will never grant us the peace and satisfaction that we are searching for anyway. We are called to pursue eternal pursuits.

And the true fulfillment we long for will only come by accomplishing the purpose for which we were placed on this earth—to love God, to love others, and to spread His kingdom.

Just like Jesus did.

Prayer

Father, thank You for the example You have given by sending Your Son. I want to follow in Jesus' footsteps by devoting my efforts to eternal matters rather than worldly games. Help me to desire to accomplish Your will more than I desire to fit in. And help me to value Your opinion more than man's opinion. Amen.

DARKNESS CANNOT HIDE THE LIGHT OF THE WORLD

Lisa Loraine Baker

"This man came to Jesus by night ..."

—John 3:2a (ESV)

I have a precious group of writer friends. Because of our first meet-up, we call ourselves the Monketeers (something about a line of monkeys riverdancing). We text every day and share prayer requests, silly stuff, and celebration-worthy news. But because we are writers, we often share a message that reads, "I'm going dark. I'll check in later." It means, "This girl's gonna get some writin' done."

Nicodemus came to Jesus with his questions by night; daylight didn't afford him the secrecy he desired. When we Monketeers "go dark," we are seeking God and using the gifts He has given us to address questions the world is asking. Some people are frightened or embarrassed to ask an open question about salvation (or about the Bible, Jesus, the Holy Spirit, etc.). You get the drift. They post questions online—in the dark—so they don't risk exposure. It's our privilege to write books, articles, posts, and even devotionals that God has uniquely prepared us for—to answer questions people pose in the dark (maybe behind a veil of pride or ignorance, or maybe even from a sincere desire to learn more about God).

But nothing is hidden from God. Jesus welcomed Nicodemus and surprised him with His profound answer, one from which Nicodemus shied away. As we Monketeers go dark, it is our prayer to handle God's word rightly as we proclaim the gospel to a lost and dying world ... to bring His light which overcomes the darkness. You don't have to be a writer to share the light of the world—Jesus—with people along your path; He uses everyday conversations.

Prayer

Lord Jesus, I come to You knowing You are the light of the
world. I pray Your light will permeate the darkness of all who
may fear the answers only You can give. No matter our vocation,
I pray we may all be ready to share Your goodness. Thank
You we can come to You anytime and anywhere. Amen.

BAD GIRL, GOOD NEWS

Alice H. Murray

"Then, leaving her water jar, the woman went back to the town and said to the people, 'Come, see a man who told me everything I ever did. Could this be the Messiah?'"

—John 4:28–29 (NIV)

How bad was she? The Samaritan woman was so bad she was shunned by her community. People looked down on her and condemned her lifestyle.

This woman arrived at the well in Sychar alone at noon. While other local women went in groups to draw water earlier in the day, she intentionally came during the hottest part of the day to avoid contact.

But the Samaritan woman's waterpot went unfilled because of a radical encounter with a male stranger. John tells us it was a thirsty Jesus she met at the well. Jesus spoke with her and asked her to give Him a drink. While that situation doesn't seem radical today, women in biblical times simply did not speak to unknown men in public. And Jesus was a Jew, while the woman was a Samaritan; these two groups hated each other.

Even more radical were the topics of their conversation. Jesus mentioned the woman's checkered past. He noted she'd had five husbands and wasn't married to the man with whom she was living. The two discussed living water, eternal life, and the expected Messiah. Jesus divulged to this outcast foreign woman that He was the Messiah.

Excited about what she'd just heard, the woman abandoned her waterpot and returned to the city. She proclaimed the story of the man who knew all about her to all she met. And many came to believe in Jesus from this bad girl spreading the Good News.

Why would a foreign woman with a tarnished reputation be the first person to whom Jesus revealed He was the Messiah? Her story makes clear the Good News is for everyone. Yes, even foreigners, people of low social standing, and bad girls. Her circumstances reveal the extraordinary influence the Good News can have in a person's life, and that God can use anyone to tell of Him, including a social outcast.

Prayer

Dear God, forgive me for thinking I'm "too bad" to be used by
You to spread the Good News. Give me the same enthusiasm
and desire to share that the Samaritan woman had. Amen.

AN ABUNDANT LIFE

Josie Siler

"A thief comes only to steal and kill and destroy. I have come so that they may have life and have it in abundance."

—John 10:10 (CSB)

We all know that life here on earth can change in a moment. That's exactly what happened to author Beckie Lindsey when doctors diagnosed her with stage 4 ovarian cancer. Those are hard words to hear. They're even harder when doctors don't give you much hope. The prognosis was grim, yet Beckie held out hope because she knew that nothing is impossible with God.

After Beckie got the news, she went to God. She knew what the doctors said about her chances, but she wanted to know what God said. Through much prayer, Beckie heard from God. He impressed upon her spirit that He was going to heal her. These were the words Beckie counted on when the treatments began. God was right there with her through the chemo, the sickness, and the pain.

Satan never lets a good battle go unfought. He loves to whisper lies when we're at our lowest. He does everything he can to bring us down and make us turn from God. He kills and destroys.

But God.

Jesus said in John 10:10, *"I have come so that they may have life and have it in abundance."* Beckie learned it's possible to live an abundant life, even while going through cancer treatments. Even when she lost her beautiful hair. Even when she was in incredible pain. God was working. He was healing and He was encouraging. He filled Beckie with hope and joy, even when the doctors told her the prognosis wasn't good. God was also there when doctors told her she was in remission. He's still with her through tests, checkups, and maintenance drugs.

Through her journey with stage 4 ovarian cancer, treatment, and remission, Beckie learned to cling to the truth of God instead of the lies of the Evil One. We can follow her example and learn to live an abundant life in the midst of the difficult circumstances we face in life.

Prayer

Dear Lord, thank You for Your faithfulness. Thank You for peace in the midst of trying times. I'm so glad that nothing is impossible for You. I'm so glad You don't waste our pain, but can use everything for our good and Your glory. It's mind-boggling to think we can live an abundant life amid the suffering here on earth, but we can—and it's all because of You. Thank You, God! Amen.

BE WITH JESUS

Josie Siler

*"When they observed the boldness of Peter and John and realized
that they were uneducated and untrained men, they were
amazed and recognized that they had been with Jesus."*

—Acts 4:13 (CSB)

It's stressful when we're asked to do things we don't think we can do. Yet it's in those situations where God is glorified and we grow the most. Imagine how the disciples felt when Jesus told them they would do what He did—and even greater works (John 14:12–14). Talk about feeling unprepared. Sure, they lived with Jesus. They watched Him every day. They saw what He did. They even got to participate sometimes. But to do the works of the Lord on their own? That must have seemed like too much.

But then it happened. The disciples were on their own and it was their turn to do the works of the Lord. One day, Peter and John caused a ruckus in the temple after they healed a man in the name of Jesus. Crowds flocked to them and Peter preached a powerful message. About five thousand men believed that day—and Peter and John were arrested.

The next morning, powerful religious leaders gathered to question them. Peter was filled with the Holy Spirit and again boldly spoke the message of Jesus to those gathered. The religious leaders were amazed at the knowledge of these simple men and recognized that they had been with Jesus.

We're also called to tell people about Jesus. This may seem overwhelming and scary, but the Holy Spirit lives in us too and can give us the words to speak. We can be recognized as people who have been with Jesus. We don't need fancy training or a certain type of personality. Oh no, we just need Jesus!

We can find the courage to point others to Jesus by spending time with Him, just like Peter and John did. Even though we're ordinary men and women, others will be able to see that we've been with Jesus.

Prayer

Lord, thank You for helping me do things I never imagined I could
do. Help me to find more time in my day to spend with You. I
want to make that a priority so others will be able to see You in me.
Help my life to glorify You and help me to be like Jesus. Amen.

CHANGED FROM TOP TO BOTTOM

Victoria Duerstock

"... We sat down and spoke to the women who had come together. One who heard us was a woman named Lydia, ... The Lord opened her heart to pay attention to what was said by Paul. And after she was baptized, and her household as well, she urged us, saying, 'If you have judged me to be faithful to the Lord, come to my house and stay.' And she prevailed upon us."

—Acts 16:13–15 (ESV)

The progression of Lydia's life—from previously unconverted and living for herself to opening her home and offering it in service—provides us a great example of what hospitality looks like. One of my core beliefs about the life-changing truth of the gospel is that when we are converted, we are changed from top to bottom.

Considering this change, we are motivated by a pure and unbridled desire to share the Good News of the gospel with as many people as we can. And our homes can be just the avenue—the platform, the tool—God will use to allow us to reach out and invite others in.

Don't you see it? God doesn't give us what we have today to keep us comfortable and satisfied. Rather, He provides for our needs, even giving us more than we ask or need, so that we will turn and share with those around us, using it for His glory. Our talents, our dreams—and yes, even our homes—open doors to a world who needs to know Jesus and the beauty of salvation for all who hear and believe.

Prayer

Lord, make me willing to open my doors and invite
others in (no matter what my mess or lack may be)
because of the Good News that they need to hear.

TURNING THE WORLD UPSIDE DOWN

Victoria Duerstock

"And Paul went in, as was his custom ... saying, 'This Jesus, whom I proclaim to you, is the Christ.' ... But the Jews were jealous, and ... they dragged Jason and some of the brothers before the city authorities, shouting, 'These men who have turned the world upside down have come here also ...'"

—Acts 17:2–7 (ESV)

This is perhaps one of my all-time favorite sentences in Acts—"These men who have turned the world upside down have come here also."

Have you ever wished that people would say something similar of you? Ever wanted to have such a notable faith story and testimony that you are known as turning the world upside down for Jesus? And further, that wherever you go, the same will be true among the people you are with?

Oh, I long for this to be said of me, I really do. I want my faith to be so recognizable that when others see me coming, they say, "Here comes that Jesus girl who thinks she can do anything God calls her to. The girl who believes that God will accomplish the impossible—and might even use her to turn the world upside down." What kind of impact could we have in life if we really believed God could use us in this way?

What glorious joy it is to chase after Jesus and do His will. Paul and Silas were often subjected to physical beatings, prison, and more, yet their unyielding testimony impacted a world desperate for Jesus. May my life do the same thing today.

Prayer

Lord, give me eyes to see what I can do for You if only You
forge my path and give me the strength to do it.

SILENT DESPAIR

Lisa Loraine Baker

*"... that they should seek God, and perhaps feel their way toward Him
and find Him. Yet He is actually not far from each one of us ..."*
—Acts 17:27 (ESV)

Each living soul yearns—even screams—for God, who is never absent.

My dad's mom emigrated to the US from Romania when he was a baby, leaving his father behind. When Dad was five, Grandma took him back to Romania to leave him with his father. Dad cried incessantly, so his mom brought him back to the States.

After a troubled youth, Dad chose to assuage his fatherless grief by joining the Navy. Dad's ship developed engine troubles, and they limped into Pearl Harbor on December 8, 1941. Dad saw horrors he wouldn't speak of, until one evening—at a baseball game, of all places—he surprised Mom and me. I'd asked him if he'd seen a new WWII movie. He replied, "I don't need to see it. I lived it." He related some of the horrors he saw, and the reason for his quiet desperation was now unveiled.

After I surrendered to Jesus, I shared the good news with Dad. I took him to church service once, and he cried as he shared his fatherless life with a small group. I kept proclaiming the gospel to him, but he often grew belligerent and screamed at me. He said, "I pray every day! But God is losing. The devil is winning." Dad prayed the same prayer each time in Romanian. I discovered later it was the Lord's Prayer.

Fifteen years after Mom died, Dad lived in a nursing home, in and out of lucidity. I knew it was time to make another push. As I drove to the facility, I prayed, "Lord, I commit my earthly father to You. Please give him clarity so he may hear and surrender to You as Lord." Ten days before he died, my stubborn father surrendered to Jesus in the presence of my pastor, my friend, and me—his little girl. Dad now knows God as his Good Father who is always near to us.

Prayer

Father God, You are a good Father and I thank You for
always being near. You loved us enough to send Jesus to die
in our place so we may be with You forever. Amen.

FOLLOW YOUR CALL

Hope Bolinger

"… and because (Paul) was a tentmaker as (Priscilla and Aquila) were, he stayed and worked with them."

—Acts 18:3 (NIV)

"I feel discouraged," my friend told me as we perused a gift shop in Amish Country in Ohio. "I told a person who works at my church about my job, and he seemed to imply that I wasn't doing as much kingdom work as him because my job wasn't directly related to ministry."

I chewed on my lip as I held up a scarf from the shop. Tensions had risen between my friend and this church employee because the church employee had dedicated his whole career to ministry. Meanwhile, my friend served as an accessibilities coordinator at a university (meaning he provided accommodations for students with disabilities).

"Okay." I blew out a breath and put down the scarf. "Do you regularly have conversations with coworkers and students about faith?"

"Yes."

"And do you seek to glorify God through working to the best of your ability to provide accommodations? And showing the loving kindness of the Lord to the students?" I waited for his nod. "And did you feel called to this career?"

"Yes. The Lord did make it clear that He opened the door."

"Then there is no 'better' job. You're both working for the kingdom, right?"

Jesus did carpentry. Paul, for a time, made tents along with Priscilla and Aquila. Lydia sold purple-dyed fabric. All brought many to salvation. Friends, continue to follow your call. God can use you in any job or life position to bring Him glory.

Prayer

Jesus, I can often feel like a "bad Christian" because I don't spend time doing ministry 24/7. Remind me that You've purposely placed me in my calling right now and that I can uniquely lead others to You in this position. Amen.

CALLED TO MENTOR

Michelle Medlock Adams

"I always thank my God for you because of his grace given you in Christ Jesus."

—1 Corinthians 1:4 (NIV)

I am thankful for the brilliant people God has placed in my life to help me get to that next level–professionally and spiritually. Too many people today are so concerned with "making it" that they'll use you as a rung as they climb the ladder of success. But then there are those priceless individuals who will patiently teach you and encourage you to step outside your comfort zone to accomplish more than you thought possible. Those rare treasures are called mentors.

I've had different mentors during the various seasons of my life, but there are two who really invested in me and made a difference. During my stint as a sportswriter at a daily newspaper in Indiana, I was blessed with my first mentor, Bob Bridge. He taught me that every person has a story, and that every story is important. He is still the best writer I've ever encountered, and I continue to study his leads, descriptive language, and voice.

When I took a job as a magazine writer for a Christian publication in Fort Worth,

Texas, I met my second mentor, Ron Jordan. He carefully guided me as I learned to ghost-write, which was a completely new concept for me. But of all the things I learned from Ron, one stands out: He was a living demonstration of "leading by serving." He served others on staff without any expectation of recognition, so we all followed him willingly. I've never forgotten that life lesson, and I try daily to follow his example.

Because now it's my turn. And it's your turn too. God is calling us to mentor others. Mentoring is a biblical principle. Elijah mentored Elisha; Eli mentored Samuel; Mordecai mentored Esther; Jesus mentored the twelve disciples. And there are many more examples.

Investing in others may not be common in this supercompetitive world, but we are called to be uncommon. We are called to love others as we love ourselves. We are called to serve. And we are called to mentor.

Prayer

Father, thank You for the mentors You have placed in my life.
I pray that You bless them today. And Lord, help me to invest
in others and be that mentor in someone else's life. Amen.

NOBODIES

Michelle Medlock Adams

"Take a good look, friends, at who you were when you got called into this life. I don't see many of 'the brightest and the best' among you, not many influential, not many from high-society families. Isn't it obvious that God deliberately chose men and women that the culture overlooks and exploits and abuses, chose these 'nobodies' to expose the hollow pretensions of the 'somebodies'?"

—1 Corinthians 1:26–31 (MSG)

I love the song "Nobody" by Casting Crowns. I especially like the line that says, "You picked twelve outsiders nobody would have chosen, and You changed the world."

People were probably quite surprised that Jesus didn't surround Himself with church leaders, wealthy supporters, or powerful politicians. Rather, He chose twelve humble people—mostly fishermen, with a tax collector to boot. Sure, Jesus could have chosen more educated and influential men to be His disciples. But He didn't.

It's a pattern we see over and over again in the Bible: God choosing people with little status, education, or wealth to participate in important tasks for the kingdom. Why do you think God does that?

In 1 Corinthians, Paul says that God chooses the "nobodies" to show that everything good comes from Him. People with power and influence can try to claim that they get all of their success on their own—and others will believe them. But only someone with a humble heart can credit the amazing things that happen in their life to God's goodness and power. When God works in the life of someone without anything else to boast about, it gets people's attention. In other words, God gets the glory.

Maybe you feel a bit like one of the disciples today—unqualified, a little rough around the edges, but totally sold out to Jesus. That's okay. In fact, it's the perfect combination for God to use you mightily for such a time as this. God loves you and wants to use you, and that makes you a somebody.

Prayer

Lord, thank You for choosing me even though I feel unqualified. Let everything I do be a testament not to my abilities, but Yours. Amen.

PLANTING SEEDS OF FAITH

Felicia Ferguson

"I planted, Apollos watered, but God gave the increase."

—1 Corinthians 3:6 (NIV)

This verse, written by Paul to the Corinthian church, has resonated with me ever since I first read it. Ultimately, it became one of my life verses, giving me perspective on my role and growing my trust in God's work and plan. However, it wasn't until I watched a sermon by Craig Groeschel that I truly felt its impact.

Groeschel is a pastor with a checkered past. He grew up in church, but (like many teens) pretty much abandoned his faith in college. In his sermon, he relayed the story of how his fraternity had been sanctioned and, needing to change the community's perspective of them, he decided to host a Bible study with the brothers.

The problem was he didn't have a Bible, which is a necessity for that type of meeting. He said he was walking to class when he realized this, and he threw a thought toward heaven about needing a Bible for the meeting that night. When class was finished, he walked out the door … and guess who stood in the hallway? A man named Mike, who was with the Gideons. And they were handing out Bibles.

Now, that is goosebump-raising enough. However, as the old TV ad assures, "But wait, there's more!" Craig turned his life back to God through that Bible study and is now the senior pastor of Life.Church. His church created the YouVersion Bible app, which now has millions of downloads.

One Gideon Bible, a heart ready to return to faith, and the blessing of God on both led to an unimaginable increase. I doubt Mike the Gideon had any sense of what his small, simple act would create. He might even have wondered why he was doing what he was called to do, handing out Bibles to college students.

Sometimes we wonder if we are having any impact on this world. We can become frustrated when we don't see the fruit from our labors. But our actions can be like Mike's: simple, heartfelt obediences that are a single, but important, step in God's overall plan.

Prayer

Lord, help me to see my small words and actions
as part of Your greater picture. Amen.

TREASURE IN JARS OF CLAY

Victoria Duerstock

"For what we proclaim is not ourselves, but Jesus Christ as Lord …
For God, who said, 'Let light shine out of darkness,' has shone in
our hearts to give the light of the knowledge of the glory of God in
the face of Jesus Christ. But we have this treasure in jars of clay, to
show that the surpassing power belongs to God and not to us."

—2 Corinthians 4:5–7 (ESV)

The weakness of our human flesh can be discouraging at times. Our frailty, though, is the perfect canvas for God to work. Because we have light to share—the truth of the gospel to a lost and dying world—we should live our lives in service to Him who has saved us. But we grow tired and weary and often lack the will to pursue this goal with intention.

More than that, as the rest of this Scripture passage reflects, we "are afflicted in every way, but not crushed; perplexed, but not driven to despair; persecuted, but not forsaken; struck down, but not destroyed; always carrying in the body the death of Jesus, so that the life of Jesus may also be manifested in our bodies" (2 Corinthians 4:8-10).

Sweet friend, I hope that you will change your perspective on your lack today. Weak vessels are the perfect backdrop for God's greatness to be on full display. When He is at the forefront, then the glory goes to Him. If we are capable of service on our own, then there is nowhere for Him to show up and shine through us.

Instead of relying on our own abilities, talents, and resources, we might just live life more fully and abundantly if we dared walk outside our comfort zone. Imagine what He might see fit to do through you and me if we knew it had nothing to do with us, and everything to do with Him.

Prayer

Lord, remind me today to be willing to risk it all
beyond my area of comfort to serve You. Please show
up and do more than I can ask or think today!

FOCAL POINT OF OUR GAZE

Tessa Emily Hall

*"So we don't look at the troubles we can see now; rather,
we fix our gaze on things that cannot be seen."*

—2 Corinthians 4:18a (NLT)

A man named Nik Wallenda is known for achieving daredevil and nearly impossible feats—such as walking along a tightrope over the Grand Canyon and across Nicaragua's Masaya Volcano. Although I don't necessarily think that's wise, nor do I advise trying it, I do applaud him for praising Jesus as the source of his victory. He claims to rely on God's strength and peace to keep him stable every step of the journey.

This must've been the same peace that held Peter above the waters as he, too, attempted the impossible by walking along the stormy sea. But he learned his lesson the hard way.

When Peter looked away from the source of his peace, what happened?

I think you know the answer.

In life, God may call us to step out into treacherous waters as well. (I hope the consequences aren't as fatal as Nik's could be!) As we take that first step of obedience, where will we plant our gaze? If we focus on the impossibility of the situation, then we are doomed to fall from either fear or pride.

But if we draw strength and peace from Christ, then we can trust that He will keep our heads above the waters ... as long as we remain focused on Him.

Prayer

Lord, when You call me to take steps of faith, give me the boldness and peace I need to stay afloat. Rather than looking at the chaos around me, help me to lift my eyes to You instead—the source of my victory. Amen.

FAITH IS THE KEY

Tessa Emily Hall

"For we live by believing and not by seeing."

—2 Corinthians 5:7 (NLT)

Most people nowadays have a spare car key on hand. But if they don't have a spare and accidently lock themselves out of their cars, they'd give the locksmith a call.

My granddaddy, however, had another solution.

This event occurred when my grandparents were college students. I'll let my grandma share it in her own words …

One afternoon, we drove to the park to study for exams. When George announced we had to leave so as not to be late for the church evening service he was scheduled to preach at, he found out he had locked the keys inside the car. We tried to no avail to figure out a way to unlock the door.

We decided we would have to break a window.

Then suddenly, George announced that God could unlock the door … if we prayed.

Well, this was George's faith—not mine. I hesitated. He said, "Let's fold up the blankets and get our books—if we believe."

So I did, reluctantly. George prayed a short prayer—opened the car door—and we got in. Granddaddy knew God's power was greater than that of a locked door.

I wonder how many times I've limited God by placing too much faith in the rules of laws and nature. Yet God isn't bound by what we can see.

Logically, my grandparents needed a key. But it was Granddaddy's faith that unlocked the door instead.

That's how powerful our faith is.

Actually, no. That's how powerful our *God* is.

Prayer

Lord, You are not limited by what I see in the natural world. Give me faith to believe that You can accomplish the impossible in my life. Amen.

GOD MAKES ALL GRACE ABOUND TO YOU

Melanie Redd

"And God is able to bless you abundantly, so that in all things at all times, having all that you need, you will abound in every good work."

—2 Corinthians 9:8 (NIV)

Over the past few months, my mom has spent a lot of time in the hospital and at doctor's offices. She is feeling much better now, but the majority of our summer was spent around doctors, nurses, and physical therapists.

One of these caregivers was a traveling nurse from Florida. Her name was Lauren. We only encountered her once as she was working a twelve-hour weekend shift and caring for my mom. During the last hour of her long shift, my mom asked her if she would help her to comb her hair. That sweet nurse began to comb my mother's hair very carefully. (Due to the nature of my mom's surgery, the rest of us were afraid to upset her head wounds.)

In those early morning moments at the hospital, I got to see the most beautiful picture of God's grace abounding to us. The simple act of styling a sick woman's hair blessed us that day.

God's grace is like that. It comes in so many forms—a kind text message, a hug, lovely flowers, a breeze on a hot day, an unexpected check, a good word, a promotion, time with friends, and even laughter.

Truly, God makes all grace abound to us. He gives us all we need, at all times, so that we may do what we need to do. We can confidently step into this day because God promises to make all grace abound to us.

Prayer

Lord, thank You for Your incredible grace in
my life. Help me to enjoy it today!

LIMITLESS

Lori Scott

"But he said to me, 'My grace is sufficient for you, for my power is made perfect in weakness.' Therefore I will boast all the more gladly of my weaknesses, so that the power of Christ may rest upon me."

—2 Corinthians 12:9 (ESV)

As a type 1 diabetic, I have limits. I avoid certain foods because they push my blood sugar too high, causing excessive thirst, fatigue, and other problems. When my blood sugar drops, it causes double vision, slurred speech, and cognitive problems such as forgetfulness, limiting my ability to communicate. Sudden changes in blood sugars can sideline me at sporting events or cause me to pass out.

I am restricted by my chronic illness. Perhaps you are likewise restricted, either by a chronic illness or some other barrier.

Take heart. Our limitations do not define us. God does. And He calls us His children (1 John 3:1) who are perfectly and wonderfully made (Psalm 139:14).

Consider the apostle Paul. Tradition says that the "thorn in the flesh" he suffered from was a major eye issue. Maybe his weakness kept Paul humble. Maybe it made him more relatable. At the very least, the situation forced him to rely more on God's strength, which is what suffering can accomplish in all of us if we allow it to.

For those of us who are plagued with chronic illness and question why we were created this way, remember—God doesn't make mistakes. He has a plan for all of us. What the world may view as a flaw is the very thing that makes us uniquely equipped to do what God has called us to do. When we are in a position of weakness, God will carry us, if necessary, and allow us to do hard things. Then, His power becomes evident to the people around us. Because of struggles we have endured, we can touch the lives of others.

With God, what we can accomplish is limitless.

Prayer

Lord, give a new perspective on my weaknesses. Let me rely
on Your strength each day to serve You to the best of my
ability. Help me reach beyond my limitations. Amen.

CAN YOU SEE CHRIST IN ME?

Lisa Loraine Baker

"And they glorified God because of me."
—Galatians 1:24 (ESV)

Esther is a vivacious, seventy-seven-year-old widow who is staying busy to assuage her grief. Every morning, this godly woman prays, "Lord God, please show me how to bring You glory today. Show me an open door so I may share Your goodness."

Esther drives a church member to dialysis three times a week. While she waits, Esther reads her Bible or Christian Living books. Even while reading, Esther is quick to start a conversation with another person in the waiting room or in a nearby fast-food restaurant.

During one stop, Esther asked the clerk if they could make mild cheese sticks for her because her system can't handle spicy food. The clerk dismissed her "off the menu" request, so Esther asked for coffee and turned to take a seat. As she turned, she was almost nose-to-nose with a man whose appearance said "I'm homeless."

He overheard the clerk's remarks to Esther and barked at the clerk, "Get this woman what she'd like. You know you can make it. And don't say you don't have time. I'm the only other person here."

The clerk promised he'd make the mild cheese sticks and bring them to Esther when they were ready. Esther thanked him and ordered a coffee for her benefactor. As the gruff man took a seat, Esther carried the cup of hot coffee to him and thanked him. Embarrassed by his behavior, the man spilled his story. He spoke of the loss of his family and of his music he loved so well.

Esther usually carries a Christian book with her in case she meets someone in need. That morning, she'd grabbed a CD instead—a CD filled with her favorite hymns. As the man shared his loss, she smiled and told him she knew the Lord had her bring the CD just for him. His tears were the only acknowledgement she desired, and she knew the Lord used her that day so the man could see Christ at work. May we do the same.

Prayer

Father, I know You never slumber nor sleep. I am in awe of
You and how You provide blessings to us—and to "the least of
these"—when we obey. Thank You for allowing me the privilege
of bringing glory to You by how You use me every day. Amen.

BURDENS

Lori Scott

"Carry each other's burdens, and in this way you will fulfill the law of Christ."
—Galatians 6:2 (NIV)

Loss. Regret. Divorce. Death. Our heartaches can sometimes feed into compromised mental health. But people dealing with these emotions often hide their pain because of the stigma attached to temporary or ongoing mental illness, such as depression or chronic anxiety.

The problem is that without visible scars, others may not recognize a person's wounds. Which can lead to more despair.

It's like lifting a couch. You might be able to do it alone, but it's an easier task when someone holds the other end. That's the idea behind sharing each other's burdens. When you hurt, I hurt. When you cry, I cry. And when you struggle, I'm right beside you, lifting you up.

Easier said than done, right?

Or maybe not. Consider Barnabas' role in the Apostle Paul's life. Paul brutally persecuted Christians until he had an encounter with Jesus on the road to Damascus. When

Paul realized Jesus was who he claimed to be—the Son of God—he switched sides. So impactful was his conversion that Paul dedicated himself to be a follower of the very faith he tried to eradicate. However, believers didn't trust his change of heart and shunned him, perhaps thinking this was a trick.

Imagine Paul's regret. Guilt. Isolation.

He might have stayed in that miserable state had Barnabas not intervened. Barnabas not only stood up for Paul but also traveled with him. Barnabas' encouragement enabled Paul to carry out his ministry. Barnabas shared Paul's burden.

Someone once drove this point home for me when they said, "Thank you for listening. Even though I feel like I'm carrying the weight of the world, at least I don't have to carry it alone anymore."

Wow.

So the next time you encounter a person struggling with depression or anxiety, listen to them. Encourage them. And pray.

It might not seem like much, but for them, your presence and care might change their world.

Prayer

Lord, make me sensitive to the needs of others. Equip
me to walk with them through their hurt and give me the
time to be Your hands and feet to them. Amen.

YOU WERE CHOSEN!

Melanie Redd

*"For he chose us in him before the creation of the world
to be holy and blameless in his sight. In love ..."*
—Ephesians 1:4 (NIV)

I grew up in a neighborhood with almost all boys. There were a couple of girls, but they were younger than me. So I did what any other elementary-aged girl would do—I hung out with the boys and did what they liked to do. From kickball to football to tag to hide-and-seek, we played outdoors all the time and had so much fun.

Often, our play required choosing teams. Two of the kids would serve as captains, and the rest of the kids would be chosen—one at a time—to play on a team. Everyone loved to be chosen. Everyone looked forward to hearing their name called out.

Did you know that God also chooses us? Before the world was even formed, the Lord chose you and me. He called our names! And God invites us to follow Him in holiness and in clean living. No, I can't perfectly explain choosing and predestination and calling to you—but I can tell you that, if you are reading these words and are in a relationship with the Lord Jesus Christ, you were chosen! You are chosen! He hand-picked you and you accepted His call on your life.

What does this mean for you? It means you can walk in courage and boldness, knowing you have been selected for God's team. He knew before the foundations of the world that you would hear and respond to His call. He adores you and has amazing plans ahead for your life.

Prayer

Embolden me, Lord! I want to walk courageously with
You in my calling. I want to serve You gladly and be a
faithful and valuable member of Your team.

BEYOND ALL LIMITATIONS

Michelle Medlock Adams

"Never doubt God's mighty power to work in you and accomplish all this. He will achieve infinitely more than your greatest request, your most unbelievable dream, and exceed your wildest imagination! He will outdo them all, for his miraculous power constantly energizes you."

—Ephesians 3:20 (TPT)

In any children's Sunday school classroom, one of the first stories you'll likely hear is the story of baby Moses. In case you're a little foggy on the story, here's a recap (Exodus 2). The Pharaoh of Egypt had decreed that all Hebrew boy babies were to be drowned at birth, so when Yocheved had Moses, she decided to hide him to spare his life. She put him in a basket and sent him down the river, asking her daughter Miriam to watch over her baby brother from a distance. But something that's not often mentioned when this Bible story is taught is the age of Miriam. Bible experts say Miriam was probably only about six or seven years old when God used her to save her baby brother's life.

Imagine a little girl, the same age as your average first or second grader, watching her brother float down the river in a basket. Imagine her heart thumping as the daughter of the Pharaoh noticed the basket and opened it, discovering a Hebrew baby. And imagine the huge amount of bravery it took for Miriam to step out of hiding and ask the Pharaoh's daughter herself if she'd like help raising the baby.

Miriam was just a little girl, but she was big on the inside. I imagine she was driven both by her love for her brother and by everything she'd been taught about God's goodness and protection. Even as a young child, she knew she could trust God. She never could have imagined how important her act of bravery would be for the people of God!

No matter our limitations, whether real or perceived, God can still use us in mighty ways. Don't discount yourself because of your age, your lack of experience, or your short-comings. God often uses the least likely people to accomplish amazing things!

Prayer

Lord, help me to stop focusing on my limitations and see myself as
You see me. Give me the boldness to do big things for You. Amen.

GOD IS ALWAYS AT WORK IN YOUR LIFE

Melanie Redd

> *"… being confident of this, that he who began a good work in you will carry it on to completion until the day of Christ Jesus."*
>
> —Philippians 1:6 (NIV)

Have you ever read or heard a quote that really stuck with you? Something that someone shared that hit you squarely between the eyes as profound and unforgettable? One of these quotes in my life comes from author and pastor John Piper. He shared this quote on his Desiring God website and on social media.

Here it is: "God is always doing 10,000 things in your life, and you may be aware of three of them."

It's true! God is always doing a myriad of things in our lives. He is working in us, for us, around us, through us, and with us. Through circumstances, life events, people, situations, hardships, blessings, successes, heartaches, and even sickness, our amazing God can masterfully use all things to work in us and accomplish His plans for our lives.

In my life, I've seen God use the illnesses of my parents, my daughter's move to a new city, the retirement of our precious pastor, and so many more things to do profound work in my life. These losses and changes have caused me to pray more, journal more, read the Bible more, and look to Jesus more. God's wise workings in our lives will do that. They will transform us!

So how is God at work in your life? What two or three things have you seen him do?

Prayer

Lord, thank You for working every single moment in my life.
Thank You for all that You have ahead for my life. Would You
remind me to keep focusing my attention heavenward?

YES, LORD

Michelle Medlock Adams

"Not that I have already obtained all this, or have already arrived at my goal, but I press on to take hold of that for which Christ Jesus took hold of me. Brothers and sisters, I do not consider myself yet to have taken hold of it. But one thing I do: Forgetting what is behind and straining toward what is ahead, I press on toward the goal to win the prize for which God has called me heavenward in Christ Jesus."

—Philippians 3:12–14 (NIV)

Over the course of my career, I've been blessed to interview many amazing people from all walks of life, but one interview impacted me so much that I've never forgotten it. I was called upon to interview evangelist Reinhard Bonnke and write a feature piece about him. Having researched his ministry and its impact on the world, I remember asking him if he had ever felt overwhelmed or nervous about the immense call on his life. His answer astounded me.

He said that when God called him to Africa to preach the gospel, he responded, "God, why would You choose me for such a weighty assignment?" And God answered, saying: "You were not my first choice. There were two others before you, but they both said 'no.' Will you do it?" And Reinhard humbly answered, "Yes, Lord."

As a result, more than 79 million people came to Christ during his crusade ministry that lasted from 1967 until his retirement in 2017. Reinhard Bonnke has gone to heaven now, but oh, what a welcome he must've received when he passed through those pearly gates!

Let me ask you something—what would your answer have been if God had asked you to preach to millions overseas? You see, Reinhard didn't see himself as someone qualified for such a big task, but he said "yes" anyway, knowing that he served a big God.

What is God calling you to do for Him? And most importantly, what is holding you back from obeying that call? Take it from Reinhard Bonnke—just say, "Yes, Lord," and go forward in confidence, knowing that if God called you, He will equip you.

Prayer

Lord, help me to say "yes" to You, even when I feel scared,
underqualified, and small. And help me to serve You with my
whole heart, no matter what task You have for me. Amen.

LIES WE TELL OURSELVES

Lori Scott

*"Finally, brethren, whatsoever things are true, whatsoever things
are honest, whatsoever things are just, whatsoever things are pure,
whatsoever things are lovely, whatsoever things are of good report; if
there be any virtue, and if there be any praise, think on these things."*

—Philippians 4:8 (KJV)

"I love this picture you drew," my friend told me, pointing to a doodle on my notes.

Shrugging, I lowered my eyes. "Thanks. I try, but I'm not very good."

After that conversation, my daughter scolded me. "Mom, you're nice to everyone you meet, but you are so mean to yourself."

I scoffed. "No, I just view my skills realistically. I love drawing, but what I can do is nothing compared to real artists. I'm slightly above average."

"I'm not talking about art." She scowled at me. "No matter what you do, you criticize yourself, downplay your successes, and point out your flaws. Cut it out. I think you're awesome."

Awesome? I dismissed her compliment with a wave.

Still, I mulled over what she'd said. She's right—I often tell myself *You're not good enough. Not pretty enough. Not clever enough. Not ... enough.*

And I'm not alone. Some people are harder on themselves than others, but the truth is, everyone falls somewhere on that self-criticism scale.

We are our own worst enemy. And we are liars.

We can replace negative thinking with truth from the Bible. In fact, Philippians 4:8 instructs us to think about things that are true, noble, right, pure, lovely, admirable, and praiseworthy.

Change the narrative in your head and find your worth in God's word. The Bible says we are made in God's image (Genesis 1:26). We reflect the glory of God (2 Corinthians 3:18). We are valuable to God (Luke 12:7). We are precious (Isaiah 43:4).

No more lying to ourselves. If the unwavering God of the universe affirms our worth, maybe it's time we start listening.

Prayer

Lord, thank You for the talents you have given me. Help me to
use them to the best of my ability. Thank You for the face and
body You've given me. Help me honor You by caring for myself.
Thank You for loving me, even when I don't love myself. Amen.

YOU CAN DO ALL THINGS

Melanie Redd

"I can do all this through him who gives me strength."

—Philippians 4:13 (NIV)

It was so strange. We were in New Testament class in seminary when my professor shared something that was a revelation to me. I'd never heard it before. While looking at today's verse about being able to do all things through Christ, my professor made an interesting observation.

He explained that when this oft-quoted promise is mentioned, it is rarely shared in context with the verses all around it. However, when you go back to look at the verses before and after this promise, you discover that Paul was writing to the church at Philippi about his finances, his hunger pains, and some of the ways God had provided for him in his ministry. Quite simply, Paul had learned that he could do all things through Christ who gave him strength. He could be hungry or full, having plenty or nothing at all. Whether people were generous or not, he could still be okay.

So can we!

In Christ and with Christ, we can go through anything. Some days it may not feel like it. But God promises to give us all of the grace, power, rest, and hope that we need to face any challenge. What are you facing today? In what area do you need Christ to give you strength? Why not ask Jesus to be enough right now for you?

Prayer

Father, I need you! There are so many situations that get past me in a hurry. I don't want to figure things out without You. I want to calculate with You in every single equation today.

FOMO

Lisa Loraine Baker

"… and not holding fast to the Head, from whom the whole body, nourished and knit together through its joints and ligaments, grows with a growth that is from God."

—Colossians 2:19 (ESV)

I love social media. I "hate" social media. I love checking in with my friends and encouraging them when I can. I love stunning photographs, inspiring quotations, and celebrating a friend's victory. I hate, however, when I fall into the trap of *FOMO—Fear of Missing Out*—as I compare and contrast my life with theirs. We are called to grow as Christians, and I don't think our spiritual growth equates to a large social media following. Instead, it means growing in Christ, the Head of the church.

As Christ-followers, we are not to subject ourselves to *FOMO;* we are to look to Him, not the world. Social media or any other world-following entity can lure us into believing we must look like *that* person; do exciting things all day, every day; share each moment of each day; be successful; be beautiful; travel the world; be fit; etc. This brings separation, and we, as the body of Christ, are called to hold fast and be knit together *in Him.*

You know what? I'm not other people, yet neither are they me. If I take my eyes off Him and peer into the horizontal world of what-ifs and why-nots, I make it about me. Living this life as a Christ-follower, obedient to the gospel, means His church grows together. We are nourished in Him together—not as separate entities who boast about anything but Jesus.

Social media is not inherently wrong. Thinking our value lies in it, however, is. My worth is found in Christ alone, and when I focus on Him first, I lose my *FOMO* because I remember I am a child of the King of Kings and Lord of Lords.

Prayer

Lord Jesus, thank You we can hold fast to You as our Lord and
Savior. Let any growth we enjoy as Your church be in You. Help
us to remain humble servants as we boast in You alone. Amen.

PRAYER

Lori Scott

"Devote yourselves to prayer, being watchful and thankful."

—Colossians 4:2 (NIV)

Recently, I met a friend whose father, an incredible prayer warrior, had died. "Pray for me," she pleaded, tears streaming down her face. "Pray because I feel the prayer void left by his death."

I cannot imagine the loss.

Right now, I'm fortunate. Every day, my parents pray for God's guidance in my life. For wisdom to deal with stress. For healing and strength to overcome obstacles. Every day, I feel the blanket of comfort from those prayers covering my life, just as my parents experienced from the prayers of their parents.

It doesn't matter how young or how old you are. God wants us to come to Him with our requests, our praises, our doubts, and our temptations. In fact, the Bible commands us to pray without ceasing. Christ modeled this for us. In Matthew 5, Jesus tells us to pray for our enemies. In Matthew 6, He gave us what is traditionally called the Lord's Prayer. In

Matthew 7 and 21, He reminds us about the power of prayer. And in Mark 1:35, He rose early in the morning and went to a quiet place to pray.

When we follow Jesus' example, we can stand before the throne of the Almighty and blanket our loved ones in prayer.

Except when we don't.

Perhaps we get busy, preoccupied with the urgent while the eternal things wait on the sidelines. We forget the power of other's prayers for us. We forget the power of our own for them. We let distractions keep us from talking to our Father.

To keep that from happening, make daily prayer a priority. Pray in the shower. Pray on your way to work. Pray in a quiet place. Pray to fill the void in your life and the in lives of others.

Prayer

Lord, thank You for all the blessings You've brought into my life,
especially those that came from the prayers of others. Please cause your
Holy Spirit to remind me about who to pray for every day. Amen.

A SINCERE FAITH

Josie Siler

*"I recall your sincere faith that first lived in your grandmother Lois
and in your mother Eunice and now, I am convinced, is in you also."*
—2 Timothy 1:5 (CSB)

We know names like Billy Graham, C. S. Lewis, Fanny Crosby, Hudson Taylor, Charles Spurgeon, and Corrie ten Boom. But do we know the names of their pastors, the person who first told them about Jesus, or their parents? Maybe, but probably not. The people who influence the influencers often go unnamed and unknown, but their lives are no less extraordinary.

In Paul's second letter to Timothy, he begins by calling Timothy his dearly loved son. He then takes a moment to note Timothy's sincere faith and to remember that it first lived in Timothy's grandmother Lois and his mother, Eunice. This section of Scripture is often overlooked. We all know Paul was a bit wordy; many of his letters start out in a similar way. He often mentions specific people, but this time he's mentioning women of sincere faith, and that's something we should notice.

Timothy was like a son to Paul, and even though he was young, he was a leader in the church. He influenced a generation, and through Paul's letters to him, his life impacted all of us who follow the Lord. Without the faith and faithfulness of Timothy's mother, Eunice, and her mother, Lois, we would have missed out on so much. They believed first, and it was their influence that impacted Timothy—who then impacted the world!

Look around your sphere of influence. Whom can you tell about Jesus? Who can you share a story with about how God has worked in your life? Never feel like you don't matter. Your life is a living testimony and you never know who's watching.

We may live ordinary lives, but our sincere faith might influence someone who will go on to do extraordinary things … and that's extraordinary too!

Prayer

Dear Lord, some days I feel so incredibly ordinary. I look around and see other people doing amazing things, and I feel so inadequate. Yet I know You love me. I know You made me on purpose, for a purpose. I trust Your plan for my life. Help me be faithful in the big things—and the little, ordinary things—in this extraordinary life You've given me. Amen.

MOMENTS OF COURAGE

Michelle Medlock Adams

"For God hath not given us the spirit of fear; but of power, and of love, and of a sound mind."

—2 Timothy 1:7 (KJV)

On December 1, 1955, Rosa Parks boarded a city bus in Montgomery, Alabama, to ride home from her seamstress job at a local department store. Like every day, she seated herself in the "colored section," as was expected for Black passengers at the time—even though she knew she didn't deserve a second-class seat because of the color of her skin.

So when the bus driver asked Rosa to give up her seat to make room for a white passenger to sit, she refused. The driver called the police, and Parks was arrested. But that wasn't the end of *the* story or *her* story.

Rosa's act of courage inspired African American leaders, groups, and churches to continue the fight for justice. Word spread, and on December 5, the day of her trial, about 40,000 Black bus riders boycotted the Montgomery bus system. The next year, racially segregated buses were deemed unlawful under the Fourteenth Amendment. Rosa's act of bravery—standing up for herself by staying seated on that bus—proved to be a monumental step in the Civil Rights movement.

By quietly confronting injustice, one woman changed a nation.

Like Rosa, we have to face our fears and stand up for what we believe. We need to defend what's good and just, no matter what those around us say or do. But we don't have to do it alone. God has promised to never leave us nor forsake us. With His strength, we can face anything.

It's our God, the God of truth and justice, who takes our moments of courage and transforms them into something greater than ourselves. Who knows? Your one act of bravery could change this world for the better.

Prayer

Father, thank You for filling me with Your love. Help me to
stand up for what's right, even if it's not popular. Please use
my small acts of courage for Your kingdom. Amen.

BECOMING A WILLING VESSEL

Tessa Emily Hall

"Therefore, if anyone cleanses himself from what is dishonorable,
he will be a vessel for honorable use, set apart as holy, useful
to the master of the house, ready for every good work."

—2 Timothy 2:21 (ESV)

John the Baptist didn't have the greatest reputation, to say the least. Growing up isolated in the desert played a big factor in his odd appearance and quirks. The Pharisees questioned his authority to baptize people because, in their eyes, he wasn't "important."

Yet isn't it a relief that God doesn't choose us based on our popularity?

John the Baptist became one of the most well-known figures in the Bible. God chose him to be the one to prepare hearts for the Messiah.

Why?

I can imagine those lonely years John spent in the desert produced a great deal of humility in him. I wonder about the prayers he uttered—if, in the stillness of the night, John begged God to use him for His glory. Both John's life and his heart must've remained in a position of surrender and admiration to the Lord.

If you've been asking God to use you in a special way as well, then rest assured that God will answer that prayer. How do I know?

Because He's looking for people to prepare the way for Jesus' Second Coming. Yet He's not searching for strictly important, beautiful, or popular people.

Rather, God is looking for a pure heart and a *willing vessel*.

Prayer

Father, You see my heart to be used for the advancement of Your kingdom. Keep me pure and devoted to You so that I can be a vessel for honorable use, ready to carry Your message to this world. Amen.

IN EVERY WAY

Hope Bolinger

"… (Jesus) has been tempted in every way, just as we are—yet he did not sin."
—Hebrews 4:15 (NIV)

If you're going through something, someone else is too.

I live by this philosophy. Whether I vent the frustrations that hurting, unmarried people endure from their well-meaning married contemporaries, or whether I am facing a temptation and feel as though no one else has gone through the harrowing battle against this particular sin …

Someone else feels the same struggles, endures the same battles. And they need to hear that we do too.

Throughout my high school years, I struggled with assurance of salvation. Many chapel speakers had seemed to imply that if we ever had doubts, we probably were never saved to begin with—a very unbiblical idea.

I spent years struggling with this, wrestling with this. Eventually, God helped ease me through the obstacles and come to an understanding that if He promised salvation, and I accepted it with open arms, then He would do what He promised He would do.

Relief flooded me. And the situation prepared me for sitting face-to-face with a dormmate who encountered the same doubts. I told her how God helped me to overcome my own.

Tears sparkled in her eyes. "Thank you."

In that moment, I realized that the years of frustration and uncertainty led me to this moment, where I could help her.

We have a relatable God. An extraordinary God who placed Himself in an ordinary human body. Jesus—as stated in Hebrews—faced every temptation. He endured homelessness, the death of family members, starvation, exhaustion, ridicule, desertion, and so much more. Praise God that we have a God who embraced the ordinary along with us, so that we will never feel alone.

Prayer

God, the Enemy likes us to think that we have to face life on
our own. But You've proven that You endured everything, and
that means I can share any burden with You. Amen.

YES, GOD REALLY DOES UNDERSTAND

Melanie Redd

"Let us then approach God's throne of grace with confidence, so that we may receive mercy and find grace to help us in our time of need."

—Hebrews 4:16 (NIV)

Eyes clearly focused, lots of nodding, phone put away, and great attention on my words … this is how my friend Beth listens. She is a wonderful friend who always seeks to truly hear and understand what I am saying. Also, because of the many hardships she has endured in her lifetime, she listens with a certain compassion and grace that is so rare in today's world.

Compassion. Mercy. Grace. Kindness. These are traits that we all seek from our friends, family members, coworkers, church friends, and neighbors. However, they are traits that many are unable to give or enjoy freely.

Thankfully, we have a God who really does understand us. Our Savior can empathize with our weaknesses. He was tempted but did not sin. Because He understands us, we can boldly approach His throne of grace. We can spend time with Him and receive all of the mercy and grace that we need—especially in times of need.

Prayer

Lord, help me to remember I can live today in courage because I can completely rely on a God who understands. I'm so grateful that You see me, hear me, and extend grace to me!

IT'S ALL ABOUT HIM

Michelle Medlock Adams

*"By faith Sarah herself received power to conceive, even when she was
past the age, since she considered him faithful who had promised."*

—Hebrews 11:11 (ESV)

Lately, I've been studying the mighty women of God throughout history, and one that stands out to me is Sarah. Just reviewing the highlights of her life, we'd have to say: "Yep, she is a woman of faith to be studied and revered." We even have biblical proof of that because Sarah is one of only two women mentioned in the Hall of Faith chapter (Hebrews 11).

But Sarah isn't mentioned as a "Hall of Faither" because she was perfect. Nope. In fact, more than once, she doubted Almighty God and even laughed at God's plan after overhearing she would have a baby at her advanced age. Sarah was also impatient and stepped out of God's will to handle things on her own when that child of promise didn't come according to her timeline. And she was jealous and angry over her botched plan and treated

Hagar (the handmaiden she had asked her husband to sleep with in order to birth an heir) unfairly. Yet Sarah is still considered a woman of great faith.

That's comforting to me. It should be comforting to you too. It means that even when we act ugly or have doubts or get impatient and take matters into our own hands, God can still use us in great and mighty ways. You know why? Because it's not about us. It's all about Him. Only God can bring our destinies to fruition. All we have to do is trust Him to do it.

So don't grow weary in the waiting, and don't try to work it out on your own. Just trust God and know that He hasn't forgotten about you. He has a great plan for this season of your life. And no matter how many mistakes you've made or will ever make, God can still use you. Just ask Sarah.

Prayer

Lord, help me to focus on You and Your plan for my life, and not my
own failings. I trust You, God, and I know that in Your perfect timing,
I will walk in all that You have planned for me here on earth. Amen.

FROM HARLOT TO HEROINE

Michelle Medlock Adams

*"By faith the harlot Rahab did not perish with those who did
not believe, when she had received the spies with peace."*

—Hebrews 11:31 (NKJV)

I love the story of Rahab found in Joshua 2 because each time I read it, I'm encouraged that if God could use Rahab in such a mighty way, He can use me too. God didn't worry about Rahab's past, her reputation, or her questionable occupation. He looked past all of that and saw her heart—a heart that was full of faith.

So when Joshua sent his two spies into Jericho to scout out the land, Jericho's king found out about their little investigatory mission and sent his men to apprehend them. But Rahab hid the spies in her house and helped them escape. She didn't know much about God, but she knew the two spies did, and she wanted to help. And her good deed did not go unnoticed. She and her family were saved, and she ended up one of only three women listed in the genealogy of Jesus!

To everyone else, she was simply "Rahab the harlot"—almost as if her ungodly occupation were her last name. Yet God saw so much more in her! If I were writing the headline for the "Israelite Tribune," I would've written in large, bold type: "From Harlot to Heroine"—because that's exactly her story in four words.

Never underestimate what our Heavenly Father can do with someone. Even someone like Rahab. Even someone like me. Even someone like you. God often uses the most unlikely people.

Prayer

Father, thank You for looking past my shortcomings. Help me to see myself as You do and help me to fulfill the calling You have on my life. Amen.

AN ACT OF KINDNESS

Michelle Medlock Adams

*"And do not forget to do good and to share with others,
for with such sacrifices God is pleased."*

—Hebrews 13:16 (NIV)

Do you remember the story of Abigail in the Bible? She isn't mentioned too many times in Scripture, but she made a big impact because she took a chance and stepped out in faith to do the right thing—even when her husband wouldn't.

Abigail was married to a wealthy man named Nabal. He owned a lot of goats and sheep, which meant he hired out many shepherds and servants to take care of his flocks. But he wasn't a grateful man. In fact, he was known for being brutish and mean.

At the time, David (the future king of Israel) was living out in the wilderness with his men. While there, he befriended some of Nabal's shepherds and helped them watch over Nabal's property. Feeling like he'd earned it and also feeling hungry, David sent some of his men to greet Nabal and ask him for food. But Nabal refused and insulted them.

When Abigail found out, she was appalled. She knew that David's men had been kind to Nabal's workers. So without telling her husband, she collected bread, wine, sheep, grain, raisins, and figs for David and his men. Then she personally rode to David, apologized profusely for her husband's rudeness, and expressed her faith that the Lord would fulfill His promises concerning David.

Abigail's kindness and generosity saved her and her family, and ultimately opened the door to her divine destiny. Because if she hadn't intervened, David was planning to attack the disrespectful Nabal and destroy his livelihood. It was Abigail's kindness that changed David's mind.

And her kindness did even more than that. When Nabal died, David asked Abigail to be his wife. David was then anointed as king, making Abigail part of a royal family.

You see, acting in kindness not only honors God but also opens the door to God's blessing. So go ahead, be kind today! Ask God to put people in your path that you can bless every single day. It'll change their life, and it might just change yours!

Prayer

Lord, help me to be more like Abigail and walk in
kindness even when people around me aren't living for
You. Show me someone to bless today. Amen.

BEAUTY

Lori Scott

*"… What matters is not your outer appearance—the styling of your hair,
the jewelry you wear, the cut of your clothes—but your inner disposition.
Cultivate inner beauty, the gentle, gracious kind that God delights in."*

—1 Peter 3:3–4 (MSG)

One day, an allergic reaction wreaked havoc on my face. My cheeks broke out in hives; one eye swelled shut, the other puffed up in classic Igor style, and everything itched. Since I didn't know the cause of the irritant, my condition worsened as the day went on. Even medications did not bring relief.

I suffered through the weekend until Monday came. Still looking dreadful, I took a day off work. After all, I teach second graders, and I didn't want to scare them with my monstrous look.

But honestly, there was more to it. My vanity dictated that no one see me looking so ugly. I had to wait for the swelling to go down.

Except it didn't.

Not wanting to miss another day (do you have any idea how hard it is to find a good substitute?!), I swallowed my pride and went back to work.

To my surprise, my students didn't flee screaming. Instead, they were fascinated by my new look and sympathized with my plight. One girl gave me a big hug and said, "Ms. Scott, it doesn't matter what you look like on the outside. You're still beautiful on the inside!"

Oh, how humbling is the wisdom of children.

God views us that way too. He tells us our beauty comes from within. He explains how that kind of loveliness can be cultivated by treating other people with kindness and charity. By helping those in need. By encouraging and praying for others. By letting God shine through us.

Inner beauty never fades. And the best part is, it's always visible, even when your face swells.

Nowadays, when I'm feeling less than my sparkly self, I remember the lesson I learned from an eight-year-old. And I get all dressed up with my best smile.

Prayer

Lord, thank You for the unique beauty You have given me, both inside
and out. Help me concentrate more on the beauty that lasts. Amen.

FAILURE

Lori Scott

"And the God of all grace, who called you to his eternal glory
in Christ, after you have suffered a little while, will himself
restore you and make you strong, firm and steadfast."

—1 Peter 5:10 (NIV)

The first time I took my daughter roller skating, I hovered around her, catching her whenever she started to topple. My obsessive protection kept her safe but didn't allow her to improve. She finally pushed away and told me, "Just let me fall, Mom."

So I watched from the sidelines as she repeatedly crashed on her backside, crawled to her feet again, and kept going. Much as it hurt me to watch, in the end she learned how to skate.

As humans, we fall. We're impatient when we should be gracious. We judge when we should forgive. We earn bruises floundering like my daughter did in the rink.

But we learn too. Graciousness. Forgiveness. And more. The Bible says that after we suffer a while, God will restore us. He allows the struggle to strengthen us.

A good example of this is the Israelites' plight in Egypt. Talk about falls! They were enslaved by the Egyptians for four hundred years. Their hard labor included making bricks, constructing buildings, and farming. But all that heartache and sweat served them well. The endurance they developed helped them trek out of Egypt and gave them the physical fortitude to wander for forty years in the wilderness (Acts 13:18–19).

God equips us for the tasks He gives us. In the training process, circumstances might beat us down. We may stumble over and over until crawling is the only option to move forward. When that happens, turn to God and remember that He uses every fall to prepare us for our future.

Prayer

Lord, I know I am flawed. But I also know You are faithful and
full of grace. Please take my hand. Guide me. And when I let go,
forgive me and bring me back into fellowship with You. Amen.

SOURCE OF VICTORY

Tessa Emily Hall

*"But you belong to God, my dear children. You have already
won a victory over those people, because the Spirit who lives in
you is greater than the spirit who lives in the world."*

—1 John 4:4 (NLT)

I've only played on a sports team once in my life, when I was a tiny eight-year-old. I spent most of that time sitting on the bench during the basketball games. But during this one game, I was out on the court. Our team was losing.

Then, with only seconds left, we scored the winning shot—right before the buzzer sounded. Guess who scored that shot?

Yours truly.

I'll never forget the feeling of accomplishing a feat that seemed too great for me in comparison with my stature and skills.

That sense of victory is puny in comparison to how David must have felt after defeating

Goliath! First Samuel 17:4 says that this giant was a "champion." His massive frame carried heavy armor made of iron and brass.

David didn't allow Goliath's appearance to intimidate him. He knew the victory was already his. Not even a giant could stand against the mighty power of God.

As we approach trials that appear massive compared to our strength, let's remember the One who is on our side. Then, when the battle is won, He will receive the glory rather than ourselves.

After all, it's a pretty cool feeling to stand face-to-face with a challenge that seems too great—and then to come out on the other side in victory.

Yes, I'm speaking from experience.

Prayer

Lord, as I face daunting trials and challenges, help me to approach them with the same assurance of victory that David had. My confidence is in You. In the end, You receive the glory. Amen.

MISSED MESSAGES

Alice H. Murray

"This is the confidence we have in approaching God: that if
we ask anything according to his will, he hears us."

—1 John 5:14 (NIV)

The couple talking to me beamed with joy. A short while earlier, I'd handed them the newborn they'd be adopting.

"It's a good thing you never called me back about that other possible adoption opportunity a few months ago, because this baby is the perfect match for you," I remarked. The husband and wife looked confused for a moment before it dawned on them, and they smiled knowingly.

The husband then explained to me what had happened—or more precisely, what hadn't happened. Although he didn't use the word, it was plain to me a miracle had occurred.

This couple went through the emotional wringer with infertility. Although birthing biological children wasn't possible, they could adopt. The two turned to God and brought their plight to Him. Yes, they prayed He'd bless them with a baby to adopt, but they didn't stop there. The couple expressly asked God to prevent them from even hearing about any situation not in His will for them to pursue.

And God answered their prayer. When our office had a baby needing an adoptive home, I tried calling the couple about their interest in the placement. Receiving no answer at their house or on either of their cell phones, I left messages asking them to call me. The same thing happened when I called their jobs and their parents' home. When we received no response, we had to place the baby with another family for adoption.

The miracle? This couple didn't receive *any* of my messages. Sure, there could be a glitch with a cell phone, or a coworker might forget to deliver a phone message. But for *several* messages to go unreceived? That was God's doing. Why? Because that wasn't the baby God meant for them.

These believers made an ordinary request of God to look out for them; the manner He chose to do so was extraordinary. God answered their prayer by making multiple messages go missing, allowing the couple to receive His message about His will for them loud and clear.

Prayer

Dear God, thank You for the opportunity to approach You and make requests. Help me trust that Your answer will be what is best for me. Amen.

ABOUT THE AUTHORS

(In Alphabetical Order by Last Name)

Michelle Medlock Adams

Lisa Loraine Baker

Hope Bolinger

Victoria Duerstock

Felicia Ferguson

Tessa Emily Hall

Mary Holloman

Alice H. Murray

Melanie Redd

Lori Z. Scott

Josie Siler